Best
Teaching
Practices
for Reaching
All Learners

This book is dedicated to people who are in my heart—my mother and father, Daurice and George; my brother and sister-in-law, Ross and Laurie; my nephew Tye Robert; my mother and father-in-law, Helene and Joe; my brother and sister-in-law, Andy and Lisa; and my niece Samantha.

Best
Teaching
Practices
for Reaching
All Learners

What Award-Winning Classroom Teachers Do

Randi Stone

CORWIN PRESS
A Sage Publications Company
Thousand Oaks, California

For information:

Corwin Press
A Sage Publications Company
2455 Teller Road
Thousand Oaks, CA 91320
www.corwinpress.com

Sage Publications Ltd.
1 Oliver's Yard
55 City Road
London EC1Y 1SP
United Kingdom

Sage Publications India Pvt. Ltd.
B-42, Panchsheel Enclave
Post Box 4109
New Delhi 110 017 India

Printed in the United States of America

Library of Congress Cataloging-in-Publication Data

Best teaching practices for reaching all learners: What award-winning classroom teachers do / Randi Stone [editor].
    p. cm.
Includes bibliographical references and index.
ISBN 0–7619–3181–3 (cloth)—ISBN 0–7619–3182–1 (paper)
    1. Effective teaching—United States—Case studies. 2. Teacher-student relationships—United States—Case studies. I. Stone, Randi.
LB1025.3.B48 2004
371.102—dc22

                                        2003022724

04   05   06   07   10   9   8   7   6   5   4   3   2   1

Acquisitions Editor: Faye Zucker
Editorial Assistant: Stacy Wagner
Production Editor: Melanie Birdsall
Copy Editor: Cheryl Duksta
Typesetter: C&M Digitals (P) Ltd.
Proofreader: Teresa Herlinger
Indexer: Michael Ferreira
Cover Designer: Tracy E. Miller
Graphic Designer: Lisa Miller

Contents

Preface

This book surveys award-winning teachers around the country about how they reach all learners. This instant network in your hands is a one-of-a-kind educational resource.

Who Should Read This Book

This book is for K–12 educators who would like to poke their noses into award-winning classrooms across the country. How are some of the best teachers in our nation reaching students? This book puts a network at your fingertips, providing names, postal addresses, and e-mail addresses of teachers who share their strategies.

Acknowledgments

I thank all the extraordinary teachers across the country who shared their insights. Grateful acknowledgment is also made to the contributors for special permission to use their material.

About the Author

Randi Stone is a graduate of Clark University, Boston University, and Salem State College. She holds credentials in elementary education and a Master of Science in broadcast communication. She completed her doctorate at the University of Massachusetts, Lowell. She is the author of previous books with Corwin Press, including *Best Classroom Practices for High School Classrooms: What Award-Winning Secondary Teachers Do,* a best-seller and winner of a Choice Award.

About the Contributors

Cynthia Baird, Teacher
Brentsville District High School
12109 Aden Road
Nokesville, Virginia 20181
School Telephone Number: (703) 590–8040
E-mail: bairdc@pwcs.edu

Number of Years Teaching: 10
Awards: Agnes Meyer Teacher of the Year, 2002
Milken Educator, 2001

Rebecca J. Baker, Teacher
Hartville Elementary School
P.O. Box 460
Hartville, Missouri 65667
School Telephone Number: (417) 741–7141 ext. 119
E-mail: dbljabak@mail.getgoin.net

Number of Years Teaching: 23
Awards: Excellence in Teaching About Agriculture Award, 2002

Stephanie Blackburn, Teacher
Bradford Elementary School
15 Church Street
Bradford, Rhode Island 02832
School Telephone Number: (401) 348–2283
E-mail: sblackburn@westerly.k12.ri.us

Number of Years Teaching: 9
Awards: Milken Family Foundation Award, 2003

Curt Boddie, Mathematics Instructor
Manhasset High School
200 Memorial Place
Manhasset, New York 11030–2300
School Telephone Number: (516) 627–4400
E-mail: curtis_boddie@manhasset.k12.nv.us

Number of Years Teaching: 34
Awards: RadioShack National Teacher Award, 2002

Patrick Boehmer, Science Teacher
Carrington High School
100 3rd Ave. S
Carrington, North Dakota 58421
School Telephone Number: (701) 652–3136
E-mail: pboehmer@carrington.k12.nd.us

Number of Years Teaching: 22
Awards: ING's Unsung Hero Award, 2002
            NABT's Outstanding Biology
            Teacher Award, 2001

Allen R. Bone, Seventh-Grade Life Science Teacher
East Middle School
2600 Grand Avenue
Butte, Montana 59701
School Telephone Number: (406) 533–2600
E-mail: abone@in-tch.com

Number of Years Teaching: 29
Awards: Walmart Environmental Science Teacher Award, 2003
            Toyota Tapestry Award, 2002

Terri L. Boutin, Teacher/Technical Assistance Facilitator
S. Ellen Jones Elementary School
600 E. Eleventh Street
New Albany, Indiana 47150
School Telephone Number: (812) 949-4306
E-mail: tboutin@insightbb.com

Number of Years Teaching: 9
Awards: Indiana Teacher of the Year, 2002
                PNC Bank and WHAS 11 Excel Award Winner, 2001

David Brock, Science Department Chair
    Roland Park Country School
    5204 Roland Avenue
    Baltimore, Maryland 21210
    School Telephone Number: (410) 323–5500
    E-mail: brockda@rpcs.org

Number of Years Teaching: 14
Awards: Presidential Award for Excellence
                in Mathematics and Science Teaching, 2001
                American Teaching Award for Outstanding Achievement in
                Teaching Science, 1998
                Tandy Prize for Teaching Excellence
                in Science, 1998

Denise L. Carlson, Third-Grade Instructor
    Gilbert Elementary School
    109 Rothmoor Drive
    Gilbert, Iowa 50105
    School Telephone Number: (515) 232–3744
    E-mail: klc@storycity.net

Number of Years Teaching: 18
Awards: Presidential Award for Excellence in Mathematics
                Teaching, 2002
                Milken National Educator Award, 2000

Christine R. Chaney, Third-Grade Teacher
    East Side Charter School
    2401 Thatcher Street
    Wilmington, Delaware 19802
    School Telephone Number: (302) 421–8270
    E-mail: cchaney@escs.k12.de.us

Number of Years Teaching: 13
Awards: MBNA Best Practices in Education, 2002
Education's Unsung Heroes Award, 2002

Brandy Fenenga, Science Teacher
Watertown Senior High School
200 9th St. NE
Watertown, South Dakota 57201
School Telephone Number: (605) 882–6316
E-mail: bfenenga@wtn.k12.sd.us

Number of Years Teaching: 7
Awards: Regional Semi-Finalist, NASDAQ National Teaching
Award, 2002
Ciba Specialty Chemicals Exemplary High School Level
Science Teaching Award, 1998

Julie Gaubatz, Science Department Coordinator, Science Teacher
W. H. Taft High School
11600 W. FM 471
San Antonio, Texas 78253
School Telephone Number: (210) 688–6000
E-mail: Julie_gaubatz@nisd.net

Number of Years Teaching: 8
Awards: Texas Medical Association Award for Teaching
Excellence, 2003
January Feature Teacher of W. H. Taft High School
(elected by student body), 2003
Northside Independent School District Education
Foundation Grant Winner, 2003

P. J. Godwin, Science Teacher
Alabama School of Fine Arts
1800 8th Avenue North
Birmingham, Alabama 35203
School Telephone Number: (205) 252–9241
E-mail: pjgodwin@asfa.k12.al.us

Number of Years Teaching: 5
Awards: Who's Who Among High School Teachers, 2002
Disney American Teacher Award
Nomination, 2002

Linda Hickam, Sixth-Grade Teacher
Indian Creek Elementary
Olathe, Kansas 66062
School Telephone Number: (913) 780–7510
E-mail: lhickamic@mail.olathe.k12.ks.us

Number of Years Teaching: 17
Awards: Crystal Apple Award, Fox 4 News, 2002
Kansas Master Teacher Award, 2000–2001
Outstanding General Education Teacher, 1999

Ali Hickey, Third-Grade Teacher
Ralph Talbot Primary School
277 Ralph Talbot Street
Weymouth, Massachusetts 02081
School Telephone Number: (781) 335–7250
E-mail: ahickey@weymouthschools.org

Number of Years Teaching: 35

Carla Hurchalla, Schools for Success Facilitator
National Board Certified Teacher, Early Childhood Generalist
North Salisbury Elementary School
Union Avenue
Salisbury, Maryland 21801
School Telephone Number: (410) 677–5807
E-mail: churchal@wcboe.org

Number of Years Teaching: 16
Awards: Christa McAuliffe Fellow, 2001–2002

Patricia Kammeyer
Antwerp Local School
Box AA Archer Drive
Antwerp, Ohio 45813
School Telephone Number: (419) 258–5421
E-mail: kammeyer@bright.net

Number of Years Teaching: 25
Awards: Christa McAuliffe Fellowship, 2002
            Who's Who in American Education, 2002

Kathleen Kessel, Elementary Teacher
    Lincoln Elementary
    821 Third Avenue West
    Dickinson, North Dakota 58601
    School Telephone Number: (701) 456–0014
    E-mail: Kathy.E.Kessel@sendit.nodak.edu

Number of Years Teaching: 8
Awards: Milken National Educator Award, 2002

Sharon Lancaster, Primary Teacher
    Indian Hills Elementary
    313 Blane Drive
    Hopkinsville, Kentucky 42240
    School Telephone Number: (270) 887–1160
    E-mail: slancast@christian.k12.ky.us

Awards: Ashland Teacher Achievement Award, 2003

Lorine M. Lee, Science Teacher, Department Chair
    Flowery Branch High School
    4450 Hog Mountain Road
    Flowery Branch, Georgia 30542
    School Telephone Number: (770) 967–8000
    E-mail: lori.lee@hallco.org

Number of Years Teaching: 7
Awards: Georgia Science Teacher of the Year, District II,
            2002–2003, 2001–2002

Stephen Lin, Choral Music Teacher and Music Department Head
    Atherton High School
    3000 Dundee Road
    Louisville, Kentucky 40205
    School Telephone Number: (502) 485–8202 or (502) 485–8803
    E-mail: slin1@jeffferson.k12.ky.us

Number of Years Teaching: 28
Awards: Kentucky Teacher of the Year, 2002
Who's Who Among American Teachers, 2002
Jefferson District, Music Teacher of the Year, 2002

Jennifer Linrud, Fifth-Grade Science Teacher
Wichita Collegiate School
9115 E. 13th Street
Wichita, Kansas 67206
School Telephone Number: (316) 634–0433
E-mail: linrud@hotmail.com

Number of Years Teaching: 6
Awards: CIBA Specialty Chemicals Middle Level Exemplary
Science Teaching Award, 2003
AIAA Foundation Educator Award, 2002
Kansas Aerospace Educator of the Year, 2002

Deni Lynn Lopez, Teacher and Math Coach
Park View Center School
1500 Alexander Street
Simi Valley, California 93065
School Telephone Number: (805) 520–6755
E-mail: denilynn2000@hotmail.com

Number of Years Teaching: 15
Awards: National Excellence in Teaching
Agriculture of the Year, 2002
California Agriculture Educator of the Year, 2002
Jiminy Cricket's Environmental
Challenge Grand Prize Winner, 2001

Loretta Loykasek, Teacher, Department Chair,
Science; Academy Coordinator, Health and
Medical Academy
Burleson High School
100 John Jones
Burleson, Texas 76028

School Telephone Number: (817) 447–5700

E-mail: lloykasek@burlesonisd.net

Number of Years Teaching: 24

Awards: Texas Medical Award, 2003

Outstanding Biology Teacher Award, Texas, 2001

RadioShack National Teacher Award, 2000

Jeannette Lucey, Immaculate Heart of Mary, Sister,
  Eighth-Grade Teacher

St. Francis de Sales High School

917 S. 47th Street

Philadelphia, Pennsylvania 19143

School Telephone Number: (215) 387–1749

E-mail: stfdsschool@yahoo.com

Number of Years Teaching: 44

Awards: Education's Unsung Heroes, 2002

Violence-Free Youth Program Challenge Award, 2002

Pledge/Promise National Environmental Award, 1995

Coleen M. Martin, Fifth-Grade Teacher

Wilder-Waite Grade School

719 Taylor Drive

Chillicothe, Illinois 61523

School Telephone Number: (309) 243–7728

E-mail: martijl2@mtco.com or
  cmartin@dunlapcusd.net

Number of Years Teaching: 29

Awards: Wal-Mart Teacher of the Year, Peoria, 2002

Presidential Science Award, 2001

Nancy B. McIver, Family and Consumer Science Teacher

Lin-Wood Public School

P.O. Box 97

Lincoln, New Hampshire 03251

School Telephone Number: (603) 745–2214

E-mail: nmciver@lin-wood.k12.nh.us

Number of Years Teaching: 15
Awards: New Hampshire Teacher of the Year, 2002
Who's Who Among American High School
Teachers, 2002
National Educator Award, Milken Family
Foundation, 2001

Mona Sue McPherson, Teacher, Science Department Chair
Hendersonville High School
123 Cherokee Road
Hendersonville, Tennessee 37075
School Telephone Number: (615) 824–6162
E-mail: mcphersons@k12tn.net or suemcpilot@yahoo.com

Number of Years Teaching: 28
Awards: Space Educator Award, 2003
Christa McAuliffe Fellowship, 1997
Tennessee Academy of Science Award, 1991

Helen F. Melvin, Elementary School Teacher
Dr. Levesque School
P.O. Box 489
Frenchville, Maine 04745
School Telephone Number: (207) 543–7302
E-mail: h_melvin@hotmail.com

Number of Years Teaching: 33
Awards: National Semiconductor Internet
Innovator Award, 2002
SEED Developer Award, 2002
FLEET School Matters Grant, 2002

Jim Miller, Teacher of Math and Science
Cle Elum-Roslyn High School
Cle Elum, Washington 98922
School Telephone Number: (509) 649–2291
E-mail: millerj@cleelum.wednet.edu or millerion@cleelum.com

Number of Years Teaching: 28
Awards: Toyota Tapestry Award, 2002
        Woodrow Wilson National Fellowship
        Foundation Award, 1990

Wendy Miller, Teacher of Students with Special Needs
    150 Koonce Town Road
    Cove City, North Carolina 28523
    School Telephone Number: (252) 514–6466

Number of Years Teaching: 16
Awards: National Board Certified Teacher, Exceptional
        Needs Specialist, 2002
        Disney American Teacher Honoree, 2002–2003

Renee A. Moore, Lead Teacher
    Broad Street High School
    1305 Martin L. King Drive
    Shelby, Mississippi 38774
    School Telephone Number: (662) 398-4047
    E-mail: rmoore@mde.k12.ms.us

Awards: Mississippi Teacher of the Year, 2001
        Milken Educator Award, 2001
        National Board Certification (AYA/ELA), 2001

Fran Mulhern, Teacher
    Unionville High School
    750 Unionville Road
    Kennett Square, Pennsylvania 19348
    School Telephone Number: (610) 347–1600
    E-mail: fmulher@ucf.k12.pa.us

Number of Years Teaching: 8
Awards: Teacher of the Year (voted by the Unionville High School
        senior class), 2000
        Pi Lambda Theta, Educational Honor Society, University
        of Pennsylvania

Susan Okeson, Principal
Wonder Park Elementary
5100 E. 4th Avenue
Anchorage, Alaska 99508
School Telephone Number: (907) 337–1569
E-mail: okeson_susan@asdk12.org

Awards: Milken National Educator Award, 2002

Cynthia L. Pochomis, Special Education Teacher
Richardson Park Learning Center
99 Middleboro Road
Wilmington, Delaware 19804
School Telephone Number: (302) 992–5574
E-mail: Cynthia.pochomis@redclay.k12.de.us

Number of Years Teaching: 26
Awards: National Board for Professional Teaching Standards
        Certification, 2002
        Presidential Award for Excellence in Science
        Teaching, 2002
        State Farm Good Neighbor Teaching Award for
        Excellence and Innovation in Mathematics, 2001

Jennifer Rhawn, Math Teacher
Brentsville District High School
12109 Aden Road
Nokesville, Virginia 20181
School Telephone Number: (703) 594–2161
E-mail: rhawnjl@pwcs.edu

Number of Years Teaching: 8
Awards: RadioShack National Teacher Award, 2002

Laurie Richards, Teacher
Pendleton Street School
88 Pendleton Street
Brewer, Maine 04412
School Telephone Number: (207) 989–8625
E-mail: lrichards@breweredu.org

Number of Years Teaching: 12
Awards: National Semiconductor Internet Innovator Award, 2002
Pi Lambda Theta, 2001
Phi Kappa Phi, 1998

Victoria L. Richey, Classroom Teacher
Ridgecrest Elementary School
137 Ridgewood
Midwest City, Oklahoma 73110
School Telephone Number: (405) 739–1671

Number of Years Teaching: 35
Awards: National Excellence in Teaching Agriculture in the
Classroom, 2002
Oklahoma Agriculture in the Classroom Teacher of the
Year, 2002
Mid-Del Distinguished Service Award, 2002
Ridgecrest Teacher of the Year, 2001

Marc Stanke, Economics and Social Studies Teacher
Brookfield Central High School
16900 W. Gebhardt Road
Brookfield, Wisconsin 53005
School Telephone Number: (262) 785–3910
E-mail: stankem@elmbrook.k12.wi.us

Number of Years Teaching: 17
Awards: Semifinalist of National Council on Economic
Education and NASDAQ Educational Foundation
National Teaching Award, 2002
Second Place, State of Wisconsin Excellence in
Teaching Economics, 2001
Washington Mutual Inc. Distinguished Teacher Award, 2001

Michael Stanton, Third- and Fourth-Grade Teacher
Ralph Talbot Primary School
277 Ralph Talbot Street
Weymouth, Massachusetts 02081
School Telephone Number: (781) 335–7250
E-mail: mstanton@weymouthschools.org

Number of Years Teaching: 8
Awards: Milken Family Foundation National Educator Award, 2002

Rochelle Waggenspack, Eighth-Grade English Teacher
Lake Elementary
14185 Hwy. 431
St. Amant, Louisiana 70774
School Telephone Number: (225) 621–2470
E-mail: wagger@apsb.org

Number of Years Teaching: 6
Awards: Unsung Heroes Award, 2002
Ascension Fund School Impact Grant, 2002

Marcia Wanous, Elementary School Teacher
Southside Elementary
P.O. Box 159
Cocolalla, Idaho 83813
School Telephone Number: (208) 263–8864
E-mail: wanousbarn@yahoo.com

Number of Years Teaching: 24
Awards: Who's Who Among America's Educators, 2002
Idaho's Science Teacher of the Year Nominee, 1995
Chamber of Commerce Professional
Educator, 1990

Jennifer Williams, Art Teacher
Skyview High School
1303 E. Greenhurst
Nampa, Idaho 83686
School Telephone Number: (208) 468–7820
E-mail: ferretw@msn.com

Number of Years Teaching: 31
Awards: National Education Association Teaching Excellence
Award, 2000
Idaho Teacher of the Year, 2002
National Unsung Heroes Award, 2000

Lynn Williams, Kindergarten and Art Specialist
Alicia Sanchez Elementary School
655 Sir Galahad Drive
Lafayette, Colorado 80026
School Telephone Number: (303) 665–2044
E-mail: lynn.williams@bvsd.k12.co.us

Number of Years Teaching: 21
Awards: Colorado Teacher of the Year Finalist, 2003
        Superintendent's Honor Roll, Excellence in
            Teaching, 2003
        Colorado Mason's Award in Excellence in
            Teaching, 2003

Wesley Yuu, Math Teacher
Mililani Middle School
95–1140 Lehiwa Drive
Mililani, Hawaii 96789
School Telephone Number: (808) 626–7355
E-mail: wesley_yuu@notes.k12.hi.us

Number of Years Teaching: 9
Awards: Presidential Award of Excellence in Mathematics and
        Science Teaching, 2002

CHAPTER *1*

Language Arts to Reach All Learners

 Hometown Hero

Ali Hickey and Michael Stanton
Weymouth, Massachusetts

G rowing up is a difficult thing to do. For children it is important that they have dreams to follow and heroes to emulate. Our nation is rediscovering the importance of heroes and the strength and courage of everyday heroes. We began this lesson in 2001, driven by the desire to help our students understand that heroes are not only larger-than-life figures on television and radio but also those people with whom we have contact on a daily basis. Professional athletes, movie stars, and musicians are all idolized and admired by children, from those in large cities to rural towns. Our goal is to guide the students in discovering that heroes are all around us. We want our children to realize that they don't always have to look deep into the night sky to find a star; sometimes the star can be found at the kitchen table, a family gathering, or even in a classroom.

Over the past seven years we have collaborated on hundreds of lessons and projects. We work hard in identifying learning standards and finding creative and meaningful ways to incorporate them into our lessons. The Hometown Hero project is a favorite. We begin the unit by asking our students the following questions:

- What is a hero?
- Can you name any present or past hero?
- Does a hero have to look a certain way?
- Do heroes need to possess certain qualities?
- Do you have a hero in your life?
- What does this person look like?
- What qualities does he or she possess?
- What heroic deeds have they performed?

Next our classes look at and read about real and mythical heroes throughout the ages. From Hercules to George Washington to Rosa Parks, we identify the characteristics and qualities of a hero. We discuss how a hero can be male or female, young or old, human or animal. We ask our students if they know of any modern-day heroes who possess similar qualities as the ones we generated. Then we ask our students if they know of any local heroes—people from our town—who perform heroic deeds or exhibit any of our identified qualities or characteristics of a hero. We list student responses and assist in making the connection that heroes are all around us.

We want our students to know that regardless of how big their house is, what kind of car their parents drive, or whether they are straight-A or straight-C students, everyone has a hero in their life. These hometown heroes may not wear capes, but they sure look like heroes to us.

The students then go on to write about our hometown heroes. Past heroes selected include moms, dads, siblings, grandparents, aunts, uncles, and yes, teachers. This assignment is loved by every student— those working above level as well as those in special education. We covered the learning standards through this endeavor, and we were surprised by the by-products: Not only did students make academic gains, they also made emotional strides. Students realized that there are many individuals who care deeply about them, and through this project they are given an opportunity to brag about a special person in their lives. The Hometown Hero project applies to all learners because the students select the qualities he or she possesses and the heroic deeds that the hero has accomplished. There are no wrong answers as long as students justify their statements. What started out as a lesson to cover certain learning standards has evolved into a super self-esteem builder.

We let our students know that what they are about to create is something that will be treasured forever, that the words they place on the paper before them will be stored away for many years to come (a super-motivating message). The biggest challenge for many students is selecting a hometown hero for the essay. Luckily it's a challenge not because our students don't have people to choose as heroes, but rather because the students don't want to hurt the feelings of other heroes by not writing about them. We overcome this obstacle by letting the students know that the other people are true heroes, too. As proof we tell students that instead of being hurt, the people they don't select will display qualities of a hero by being overjoyed that the student's essay made someone so happy and proud. We also encourage students to write a second Hometown Hero essay as a possible solution to this problem.

At parent conferences we display the students' essays. We have had parents come in for conferences with tears in their eyes and smiles on their faces. It is a fantastic way to begin talking about the strides their sons or daughters have made in our respective classrooms.

Reading the First Day

Sharon Lancaster
Hopkinsville, Kentucky

He stood in the computer center of my primary classroom looking around with uncertainty and maybe even fear. His eyes darted to me while I talked with a parent during our Open House. School would be starting in a week, and this was the big night to come and meet your teacher and see your classroom. I smiled at him, and there was a brief hint of a grin.

As I walked over to meet my VIP (very important pupil), he looked somewhat like a deer caught in the headlights. I could tell he really wasn't sure how he was supposed to respond. I bent down to where we could be eye to eye and asked his name. He responded rather timidly. I asked him what he liked to do and what he hoped to learn this year. I will never forget those great big brown eyes looking at me and his quiet voice saying, "I don't know how to read. I want to learn how to read."

After another question or two I found out that he thought he was supposed to know how to read to go to first grade. He was very apprehensive about not knowing how to read, and I could tell he was afraid he would never learn to read. I took his chin in my hand, looked directly into his eyes, and said, "I guarantee on the first day of school you will be able to read something." He looked at me again with those enormous dark brown eyes, smiled, and said, "Promise?" "I promise," I assured him. With the solemn vow that passed between us I knew that I had to make certain he would be able to read something that first day of school. I also knew that other parents had been listening, and I could tell they were skeptical about my promise.

The first day of school arrived, and I welcomed all twenty-four of my children to the classroom. Some of them had attended the Open House, and we had met; others were seeing me for the first time. Six-year-olds have a way of remembering promises, and my little guy was no exception. He came in, wished me a good morning, and found his seat. I could tell he was just waiting for me to teach him to read. We waded through all those first day of school preliminaries, and the parents left. I told the class that I had made a promise to one of their classmates—that he would be able to read something the very first day of school. I knew I had to hook them all and begin that slow process of teaching them not only to read but also to love to read.

I found my new dry erase markers in all eight colors and began to write on the chalkboard, in red marker, the word *red*. I turned and asked the children, "What word do you think is up here?" My young man raised his hand and said tentatively, "Red?" "You are exactly right!" I said with a smile. "Now give me a high five!" I then proceeded to write each of the six color words in their respective color: blue, green, yellow, black, orange, and brown. And then I decided I would have to write the word *white* in black. I pulled this off by telling the children I was writing this color word in the opposite color and hoping that they remembered what *opposite* meant. I found out very quickly that they certainly did remember when several of them shouted out, "White!" I looked over at my new student, and he had a smile on his face that would light up a room. I knew I had piqued the interest.

It wasn't long before our curriculum specialist walked in to meet the children. I told her that my students could already read. She played right along and asked me to prove it. The children were in their glory at that minute. The color words were still on the board, and the children read them in unison. She turned to them and said, "I can't believe you all are already reading! I am so excited that we have such smart boys and girls at Indian Hills!" I told her that I had made a guaranteed promise the night of the Open House to one of the students and that I knew I had to come through. The children's confidence levels began to climb that day. I found that the color word activity on the first day of school is the hook that catches the children and makes them feel confident to tackle learning to read.

Another confidence builder with my students is being able to read to the principal, guidance counselor, curriculum specialist, or secretary. These folks do a great job of encouraging and promoting reading. I choose a child that I know has been struggling and is doing an exceptional job and send the child to read to whomever is available. The adults listen, applaud, hug, and give a treat to the child. I want every child to be able to go to the office and read for someone before the year is over. This simple activity doesn't cost anything but a little time, and the rewards for my students come back tenfold.

I recently had a parent ask me what I had done to her child. My stomach did a flip, and I could not think of a thing that I had done to help this child because she is already a good student and very well behaved. I answered, "I don't know. What have I done to your child?" She answered, "All she wants to do is read. She didn't even want to pick up a book before she came to your class. Thank you so much and please keep up whatever it is you are doing! It is wonderful to see her enjoying reading and wanting to read."

The most rewarding part of teaching first grade is knowing that when my students leave my classroom, they can read; they take with them a skill that no one can take from them.

Helpful Tips

■ I echo-read the story the first day it is introduced. I read a sentence at a time adding voice and following punctuation. I think that by modeling the correct form of oral reading the children will follow suit.

■ My students love to buddy-read. I team a pair of students: a good reader and a student who may be struggling or just needs a little help.

■ Peer tutoring is a lifesaver at times. I use peer tutoring in math, also. Sometimes all it takes is a child explaining it to a classmate for the concept to become clear. I see rewards in this for both students. The student doing the tutoring is reinforcing the skills he or she has learned, and the student who is struggling is benefiting from help from a peer.

■ Student-made sight word vocabulary flashcards help to reinforce learning. The students love making their own cards. By writing the words, students become familiar with the way the word is spelled and how each letter sounds. Our local print shops donate scrap card stock, which makes perfect flashcards.

▨   Using Technology With Struggling Readers and Writers

Carla Hurchalla
Salisbury, Maryland

As a Title 1 reading teacher, I was constantly challenged to find new and innovative ways to motivate my at-risk students to learn to read and write. Because many of my students came from homes where reading and writing were not modeled and lacked success in reading and writing, most of my students did not view themselves as readers or writers. I knew that to teach them these skills I would have to help change their attitudes about themselves and their abilities. The Authors in Residence project began with my desire to change the perceptions of my young, struggling learners. The knowledge that reading and writing are connected skills led me to find a way to encourage writing as a door into reading. With these students struggling in reading and writing, I also needed to find a way to motivate them in these areas. I knew that I had a monumental task to accomplish.

I wanted to give my students real audiences to write for, thus viewing themselves as authors. Out of this desire, I designed a program called Authors in Residence, which had several goals:

1. One goal was to team my academically at-risk students with published children's authors for a collaborative writing project taking place on the Internet and through e-mail.

2. Another goal was to have these students use Internet research skills to research their writing topic and author.

3. The third goal was to strengthen students' letter-writing and communication skills through the use of e-mail with their authors.

4. The fourth goal was to enable students to strengthen their creative and informational writing skills.

5. The final goal required the students to publish their work on a Web page on the Internet.

I knew that if I could help students meet these goals, they would become lifelong readers and writers.

To help students meet these goals, I recruited published children's authors, my rationale being that my students would be strongly motivated to read and write stories when provided with authentic opportunities to interact with published authors of children's books. I began by searching the Internet for authors of books with which I was familiar. I wrote and invited several of these authors to volunteer their time to help with the project. I was delighted when many authors accepted the opportunity to mentor struggling writers.

The students developed a rapport with their author, and together they collaborated, using e-mail, on a piece of writing to be published on the Web. Students also spent time on the Internet researching writing ideas. Through daily and weekly e-mail exchanges, a brainstormed list of ideas developed into a rough draft, which went through countless revisions, and, through collaboration, was transformed into a publishable piece of work. The students then worked to publish the piece on the Internet. By the end of the project, the students were proficient in using e-mail, had strong Internet research skills, were capable of producing a basic Web page, and were readily searching for new books to read.

Some of my students continue to e-mail their mentor author, and teachers in other grades comment about the motivation my former students have to read and write. My experience with having students collaborate with children's authors on their own writing has taught me that the only way to make reading and writing meaningful for some children is to connect the skills to real-world applications and experiences.

Helpful Tips

This project can be easily replicated in other classrooms by teachers willing to search out authors or other content experts who can work with students in needed areas. This project does not need to be limited to authors of children's books; it could also include journalists, college professors, and content specialists, such as meteorologists, archeologists, and astronomers. The options are endless. I would suggest that teachers find mentor experts in whatever field they are teaching or in any area of need. The learning experience becomes extremely powerful when, for example, a meteorologist gives expert advice to science students who are analyzing the weather and making weather maps.

This project has enabled me to see the power of the Internet as a teaching tool to motivate and inspire students. The Internet is a conduit for authentic learning with real-world purposes.

Using Physical Movement to Motivate At-Risk Students to Read

Carla Hurchalla
Salisbury, Maryland

Because many of these students are struggling in class, they find alternative, disruptive behaviors in which to engage. These disruptive behaviors make the cycle of nonlearning worse: The more students engage in inappropriate behaviors in class, the less they attend to instruction. I taught one group of six-year-olds who were particularly active and interested in engaging in inappropriate behaviors. I decided that, since they were on the move physically, I would incorporate their movement into instruction.

I developed activities that required physical movement for all aspects of reading instruction. I created hopscotch boards and used the Twister game, writing sight vocabulary words and simple sentences in the squares and circles. I had students create letters with their bodies. I photographed the letters, and then we used the pictures to spell their vocabulary and sight words. We created cheers, chants, and songs to go with words and stories. I took beach balls and wrote sentences on the balls. Students enjoyed tossing the ball to their friends and reading the sentences that their fingers ended up touching when they caught the ball. I even wrote sentences on strips and put them in filled balloons. The students then had to sit on their balloons to pop them and read their sentences. I used sidewalk chalk to encourage the students to respond to what they read. They loved having the opportunity to draw on the sidewalks of the school as a response to the literature they had just read.

Through physical engagement in reading, my students were much more focused and interested in learning to read. My experience with this group of students taught me to look for the behaviors my students exhibit and then find a way to channel their behavior into positive learning activities.

Helpful Tips

When looking for ways to make learning activities more physical, be aware of safety concerns and take necessary precautions to establish safety routines. Also, if an activity is planned that may be excessively noisy, inform your neighboring teachers as a courtesy.

▧ Educating One Child at a Time

Terri L. Boutin
New Albany, Indiana

As a nominee for Indiana's 2002 State Teacher of the Year award, I was required to submit a portfolio to the selection committee. I moved easily from section to section until I reached one requirement that left me thinking for quite some time. I had to write a one-page, double-spaced, one-inch-margined message to the teachers of America. If I had only a small amount of space to try to communicate with all teachers what I felt was an important message, what would I say? I considered many options and then decided to focus on something that I felt helped me become a better teacher.

It Begins . . .

I am a collector of quotes. I keep them posted all around me to serve as reminders of the person I want to be. I happened upon this quote from Stephen Covey (1990) several years ago, and it has consistently provided me with inspiration:

> As a teacher, as well as a parent, I have found that the key to the ninety-nine is the one—particularly the one who is testing the patience and good humor of the many. It is the love and the discipline of the one student, the one child, that communicates love for the others. It's how you treat the one that reveals how

you regard the ninety-nine, because everyone is ultimately a one. (p. 197)

I initially loved this quote because it helped me with that one child who demonstrated particularly difficult behaviors. His eyes seemed to dance, and he seemed to be always in motion, always asking questions, and always smiling. I loved him right from the start, but I also knew that he took much of the energy I needed to keep our classroom orderly and productive. His name was Michael. I can easily remember his name. I remember it because I seemed to say it over and over again. In fact, his was the first student name I learned well on the very first day of school.

I'm not sure why this quote jumped out at me from the pages of Covey's book. The school year was going well, and Michael was not presenting any major challenges to a productive classroom. But I thought of Michael immediately as I read those words. I must have known that I was getting an edge to my voice or showing that I had tired of constantly redirecting Michael. Something in me knew that something just wasn't right.

When I read this quote it reminded me to think before I responded to Michael or interacted with him or even said his name. I came to realize that it didn't matter how nice I was to the other students; how I treated Michael conveyed how I regarded them. I wondered what they thought about how I felt about them. I knew that I loved all of them and easily told them so, but did they know that? Was I sending mixed messages? It was a powerful lesson for me.

Ultimately, though, this quote has inspired me in many other ways. For example, it is a reminder that the one child is each and every child who walks through our door each day—each with differing gifts, needs, abilities, and developmental levels. It is our job as teachers to meet each student where they are and work from that place to provide what that one child needs to be successful on any given day.

We do not work in a one-size-fits-all profession. With standards and accountability, we may feel that we are being told to create cookie-cutter classrooms, but that is not the case. While our student outcomes may be standardized, how we get to that place is not. It is our challenge to customize our instruction to the needs of our children so that each of them has the opportunities that he or she deserves.

It would be impossible to meet the challenge of providing for the needs of each child without the willingness to change and grow as a professional. We must continue to seek out new understandings of best teaching practices and embrace differentiated instruction to meet the needs of the one child while educating all children.

It is also important to treat each other as the one. We must recognize and value the gifts and needs of those around us, see each other as professionals, and believe that we are the experts in the field of education. We must nurture and care for each other and for ourselves because we, too, are ultimately a one.

Helpful Tips

■ Avoid calling out a student's name to redirect attention or correct an action. While this may seem like something every teacher should already know and practice, a difficult student can cause us to use strategies we know are not appropriate.

■ Do a reality check every once in a while. While you're driving home, think back on your day. Did you have an edge to your voice while speaking with a certain student? Did you have as many positive interactions with a child as you did negative interactions? It's OK if you don't like your answers. The important thing is to make a conscious effort to do it differently tomorrow.

■ If you have tried all of your tricks with a difficult student and have no strategies left, ask for help. Some schools have a behavior support team that may be able to help you come up with a plan for your student. You may want to investigate initiating a behavior support team if your school doesn't yet have one.

■ Learn as much about differentiated instruction as you can and use what you've learned to meet the individual needs of your students. Students who are engaged and feeling successful demonstrate fewer discipline problems.

Reference

Covey, S. R. (1990). *The seven habits of highly successful people.* New York: Simon & Schuster.

Using Assessment to Drive Instruction

Terri L. Boutin
New Albany, Indiana

Our school is a school of poverty. That means that enough of our students qualify for free lunch that we feed all of them without charge. We also feed them breakfast. In the summers and during school breaks, we make sure that there is someone who will meet them in the school park to offer lunch to them. Our families are, for the most part, members of the working poor. They usually do not rely on public assistance for their income, but their paychecks do not stretch far enough to provide for all of the necessities of life. Poverty is a part of most of their lives. And it affects them in many ways.

We depend on federal dollars through Title I to fund many of our programs. We are in a time of increased accountability for schools, especially those that rely on federal funds. Ours is a schoolwide Title I school. We don't differentiate between identified Title I students and other students. They are all considered Title I students—students who are at risk for failure without intervention. Our students need more than a sit-and-get model of classroom instruction, and all students deserve the opportunities provided by quality, focused instruction based on the needs of the individual students and the academic standards to which we are held accountable.

There never seems to be enough time in the day to do all that is required of us as teachers. And now a yearly test will show whether or not we have accomplished the daunting task of providing all things for all students. The outcomes for every student are the same with the No Child Left Behind Act of 2001. What more do the legislators want? We already work hard—very hard. What we need is to work smarter. We need to make every moment count.

When I first began teaching, I conducted whole-group lessons, and then I tried to meet each individual child's needs through conferencing in reading, writing, and math. I found that there were not enough minutes in the day or week or month to keep up. After analyzing their reading tests, I found there were students with similar needs. I knew that while some of my students were still trying to get a beginning, middle, and end (in that order) in their writing, there were some students who were ready to experiment with a variety of writing techniques. I am afraid that I held back presenting more difficult concepts until I was certain that everyone was ready for them. In a school such as ours, the time when everyone is ready might never come.

If you try to teach everything in a whole-group setting, you will be presenting information that some students already know and information that other students are not ready to process. In any event, you are reaching only a small percentage of your class. This may lead to frustration and lots of reteaching when you assess what you thought you had taught. It slows down instruction for everyone, and those who need more support will probably not get the concept the second time around either.

One way to work smarter is to use a variety of assessment tools to help you plan small-group and individualized instruction based on student needs. There are a variety of assessment tools and organizers available for you to use. Schools, districts, and textbook publishers use a variety of diagnostic and assessment tools for reading comprehension. Many professional books, especially those about reading or writing workshops, are filled with ideas for organizing flexible small groups.

The important thing to remember is that you need to dedicate a specific time and create a schedule for teaching specific content areas. All of those tools and organizers can provide more frustration than organization if the attempt is only halfhearted. For example, make a commitment to a specific number of minutes dedicated to a writing workshop each day. If the school day is shortened, stick to your time for writer's workshop. If other things come up, take that flexibility and put it somewhere else. Commit yourself to the time you've set for writing.

Organize your workshop or dedicated teaching time into manageable pieces. For example, dedicate a number of minutes to a mini-lesson presented to the whole group, a number of minutes to small-group writing lessons, and a number of minutes to individual student conferences in your writing workshop schedule. If you wish to have a time for sharing, be sure to build it into your schedule and honor it every day. Again, there are many structures for a writer's workshop. Take a look at examples from some published works and make them work for you and your classroom.

To meet the many needs of your students, every instructional period needs to have many opportunities for instruction. Effective planning for this instruction must begin with assessment. I have used assessment to plan whole-group, small-group, and individualized instruction, and I describe my method in the following paragraphs.

Using an assessment tool (a test, a reading assessment, a piece of student writing, etc.), create a chart with your students' names down one side (a basic class chart). Across the top, list the skills or concepts you expect to see in the work. You might want to have a prepared checklist with grade-level state standards for writing, a list of skills and subskills for a mathematics concept, and a list of reading strategies you expect to see (all on different pages, of course). As you assess each student, choose no more than three areas to work on and place a check-mark under those skills.

Ideally, you should identify skills and concepts that the student is very close to achieving. There should be some indication that the student has at least some idea of the concept or is approximating it in some way. For example, one of my state standards is that the students will use dialogue in written stories. If a student is attempting to use dialogue in writing but is not doing it effectively or not using it to move the story along, I check "uses dialogue" next to the student's name on the class chart.

The key is to then use the assessment tool to plan instruction for the next few weeks. If you find that most of your students did not demonstrate a concept you've been working on in class, you may need to develop a short series of whole-class mini-lessons to address that skill or concept. In the best scenario, you'll identify skills or concepts that only a handful of students need to work on, which guides you to create small, flexible groups. You'll also be able to pinpoint specific skills and concepts to make your individual student conferences more focused and productive.

In this time of increased school accountability, we seem to be testing students all the time. I hear teachers complain about the requirement to assess student writing four times per year with a rubric and recording the scores on a form that no one looks at later. If that is the only use of that assessment, then it is a waste of instructional time. If, however, that assessment drives instruction and helps a teacher plan focused lessons, it is a great tool—one that should not be limited in use to four times per year. Our district now also requires us to use a standardized reading assessment tool several times a year. What a shame to waste this opportunity to plan instruction that we know our students need. If we are just following the steps of a basal textbook, we don't know if the concepts we are teaching are concepts that our students are ready for at that time or if they even need to be taught to the whole group.

Using assessment to drive instruction is working smarter, not harder. It allows us to build more opportunities for instruction into our day. It encourages us to look at each child and what the child can do as opposed to what he or she can't do. It allows us to scaffold instruction, to build on what a child knows to take them to the next level of learning, so that they can meet the standards to which we are all held accountable (Vygotsky, 1978).

Helpful Tips

■ Visit your local teacher supply store or go online to peruse and purchase some professional books on setting up a reader's or writer's workshop. The same ideas can be used to successfully set up a mathematics workshop.

■ Experiment with a variety of forms to record your assessments. The process of reflecting on the student outcomes of a particular unit of study will help you build whole-group lessons, focus your instruction, and plan your end-of-unit assessments.

■ Assess often so that you can catch areas of concern early and clear up the students' confusion.

■ Spend some time with other teachers, developing assessment tools, recording instruments, and creating ways to make flexible groupings successful and meaningful.

■ Visit classrooms that have effective workshops in place.

Reference

Vygotsky, L. S. (1978). *Mind in society.* Cambridge, MA: Harvard University Press.

Motivating Middle Schoolers

Rochelle Waggenspack
St. Amant, Louisiana

Most people are aware of how difficult it is to motivate children in school, especially when it comes to lighting the fire within middle school students. It is not considered cool for seventh and eighth graders to enjoy school assignments. It is a rare instance when a middle school teacher finds a project that sparks thirteen-year-olds' interests. It was by chance that I discovered such a project, and the motivation that this project sparked was truly amazing.

It all started when my assistant principal came to me, the student council sponsor, and asked me to get the student council involved in landscaping the cement patio recess area. Up to this point the students only had a small covered walkway to hang out at during recess. The assistant principal was able to secure funds to have a thirty square-foot cement slab patio poured and a metal roof installed to cover it. The area was very dull and boring to look at. The assistant principal wanted to have flowerbeds created around the patio to add some color. I thought this would be a great idea. After doing some thinking about it, I decided to turn it into an eighth-grade class project.

I am an English teacher, and it is not intuitively apparent how landscaping could fit into the English curriculum. Most people would associate this type of project with science. I did in fact have a few parents inquire as to why I was having the students complete this project in my English class. After I informed parents and students how this project incorporated English, science, and math, most agreed that this would be a worthwhile project to further their child's education. When I first told the students about it, they weren't too thrilled by the idea. It wasn't until I told them that they would get a day out of class to actually plant the flowers that they perked up and took interest in the project.

I invited a local landscaper to class to talk about the planning that goes into landscaping a yard. To my surprise, the kids listened attentively and asked some good questions. This was my first inclination that the students were going to get into this project. The landscaper offered his time and assistance to us throughout the project, and he really enjoyed working with the kids as well.

I first had the students do research. We spent several days in the computer lab researching plants that would thrive in our south Louisiana climate. The research tied in well to my English curriculum. I'm a big proponent of using technology whenever possible in the learning process, so after completing the research, each student compiled what he or she had found into a PowerPoint presentation. The research also connected to the science component of the project. For math, the students measured the area to be landscaped and figured out how much soil, fertilizer, and mulch the flowers needed. The students also had to draw to scale a design of their flowerbed and indicate where the plants they chose would be planted.

The students first whined about having to do all that work, but when I told them that it wasn't just busy work and that they would actually be planting the flowers, they felt like their work had a purpose and meaning. They got into their research. I knew that learning was taking place when the kids came to school and told me things like, "I told my mom that she needed to plant Indian Hawthorne bushes on the side of the house because they grow well in the type of soil we have." Those types of comments are the ones teachers like to hear; it means the students are thinking about what they are learning.

After completing the research, the students were anxious to start planting, but first we had to raise money. The students, with my guidance, coordinated two fundraisers at school. One was a slipper day, where students paid a dollar to wear slippers to school for a day. This event raised a little over $500. The second fundraiser was a carnation sale for Valentine's Day. The students sold carnations for a dollar each. Kids and teachers bought carnations for friends and family members. Heart-shaped tags were made for the students to write a message to their friends. A few students volunteered their time after school the day before Valentine's Day to tag all the carnations that were sold. On Valentine's Day I delivered the carnations around school. The carnation sale raised about $700, giving us a total of $1,200 to spend on our landscaping project.

Once the money was collected, we had a budget to give to the landscaper, who then purchased plants for us. We had crepe myrtles, azaleas, Indian Hawthorne bushes, miniature gardenias, river birch trees, and begonias to plant. The landscaper donated his time to prepare the flowerbeds and soil for us. When the beds were ready, I took each class out to plant some of the flowers. At the end of the day, the students stood back and admired their hard work. The assistant principal also ordered tables and benches for the new patio. As a tribute to the eighth graders' hard work, we purchased a marble stone engraved with *Class of 2002*. The stone was placed in the middle of the flowerbed.

Teenagers of today are regarded as lazy and unmotivated. This project affirmed that, when given the chance, teenagers can prove responsible. The eighth graders took so much pride in their work that even after the project was complete they took great pains to ensure the flowerbed was kept clean and in good condition. They were so adamant about the maintenance of the flowerbeds that if they caught anyone trespassing through the flowerbed or littering they verbally chastised the careless person, whether student or teacher. This policing behavior illustrates that with proper motivation teenagers can be responsible and respectful of others' property.

All of my students enjoyed this project because it addressed all learning styles. The visual and auditory learners did well with the research and PowerPoint presentations. The tactile learners did well with measuring and planting. They had fun doing this project, and many of them forgot they were learning in the process.

The great motivator in this project was that the students could see the payoff. After seeing the eighth graders' work, the seventh graders began asking me in the hall what they would do next year for an eighth-grade class project. Even though the landscape project was a lot of work, I thought that if the students enjoyed it so much and learned something in the process, then the planning and work was worth it. I ended up writing and getting a $2,000 grant—the Unsung Heroes Award sponsored by ING Northern Annuity—to continue the landscaping project. The class of 2003 will be landscaping the front yard of campus, learning and having fun through it all.

Helpful Tips

- The teacher should carefully plan and consider all aspects of this type of project before beginning it. The first year we did this, I planned for things as they came up. Planning this way caused some confusion. The following year was better since I knew what to expect and where I wanted to go with the project.

- The second year of the project I designed a Web quest for the project. This allowed me to completely turn it over to the students from the beginning, and they did all of the work, even contacting the nurseries to buy the plants. I even had a parent volunteer to pick up the plants from the nursery. Of course, the Web quest required me to create and find useful Web sites beforehand, but it was well worth the time and effort. The second year ran smoothly without any problems.

- I recommend sending a story about the project to the local newspaper. The students love seeing their names and work in the paper.

- A motivating project such as this doesn't have to be a landscaping project. Any project that allows students to see the results of their work and have fun while working motivates them, no matter their age. A project like this answers the age-old question, "When will we ever use this stuff?"

Inspiring a Reluctant Reader

Patricia Kammeyer
Antwerp, Ohio

Inspiring a reluctant reader is one of the primary challenges—and rewards—I meet in my classroom each year. Each fall, students who have not yet learned to love the power of the written word walk through my doorway. I begin to lay the foundation that will lead to a love of reading on the first day of the school year.

I firmly believe, and best practices dictate, that all elementary-age children need to be read aloud to on a daily basis. This is one of the most important keys to changing a reluctant reader into a voracious reader. Children who have not mastered the mechanics of reading cannot enjoy the experience of reading; they struggle so hard to make sense of each individual word that they cannot relate meaning to the words. These children may be word callers, but they are not mature enough in their skills to be called readers. These students need repeated, positive experiences with reading to bridge this gap.

When a child is read aloud to, wonderful things begin to happen. The child gets to enjoy the story in a nonthreatening manner, where all that is required of the child is to be an active listener. The risk of failure is removed, and the child can relax and enjoy the reading experience. Over time, the child makes a natural connection between reading and enjoyment. In addition, the child gets to hear you, the teacher, model what the story sounds like. The child listens to the inflection of your voice and notices that you pause and stop during the story to give clarity and emphasis to the story line. The child makes connections between the written word and the magic of a good story.

It is imperative that a variety of excellent literature be selected to inspire and hook reluctant readers. I read *Flutterby,* a book from the Serendipity series by Stephen Cosgrove, on the first day of class. This is a story about a small creature that is trying to find out who or what he is. He tries to be an ant, a butterfly, and a bee, with disastrous results. Finally Flutterby discovers he is a unique individual with a special place in the world. This is a perfect story to welcome children and let them know that they, too, are unique and accepted; they don't have to be "bees" or "ants"—just being a Flutterby is all that is expected of them. Over the next few weeks, I read more books in the Serendipity series. Each time I read, I bless additional books—I hold up a book and tell the children how much I enjoy it. This becomes the book that every child wants to borrow, even the reluctant readers.

Early in the school year, I read *Thank You, Mr. Falker,* by Patricia Polacco. The little girl in this story encounters reading difficulties and is mistreated by her classmates because of this disability. At the end of the story, it is revealed that this is the story of Patricia Polacco's life. Reluctant readers see their struggles mirrored in the author's story. The discussion and sharing that follows this selection often reveal feelings of failure, hopelessness, and a desire to be and do better in reading. When the children realize that there is hope and that reading problems can be solved, they have reached a turning point. Before the school year is over, I have read all of Patricia Polacco's stories to my students. Each story is written in a child-friendly manner, and Patricia Polacco soon becomes a favorite author of my students. They begin to read her books independently because they know that between the covers of each of her books is an enjoyable experience.

By midyear, I find that my students are ready to graduate from picture books to chapter books. It is at this point that I read aloud a book in the Junie B. Jones series by Barbara Park. This humorous series is about a kindergarten child, and her experiences strike a chord in children as they remember their own kindergarten experiences. Because these books are written at a second-grade level, it is a good choice as a transition series between picture books and chapter books. The series allows children with minimal reading skills to read and enjoy a chapter book.

As their skills increase, children take a leap and read more difficult chapter books. *The Best Christmas Pageant Ever,* by Barbara Robinson, is an excellent story to read during December. Even if a child does not celebrate Christmas, he or she can enjoy meeting and hearing about the worst kids in the history of the world, the Herdmans. Elementary-age children enjoy knowing that there is good in all of us and that miracles do happen. This story lends itself to numerous supplemental activities. It is a perfect story to use with a Venn diagram, comparing and contrasting the writer of the story with one of the Herdman children. The cat is so well described in the story that it is a natural art project to have the students draw the cat. This story is also fun to have children act out for the class.

As reluctant readers become active, involved readers, it can be difficult to find a book that will challenge them and yet be provocative enough to keep their interest. John Erickson has solved this problem with his Hank the Cowdog series. Boys and girls in the classroom enjoy this series equally. The humor and adventures of Hank have children laughing so hard they can't wait to hear and then read more stories about him.

If you are willing to dedicate yourself to reading aloud to your children each day, you will find that even your most reluctant reader begins to enjoy and appreciate books. After reading the research about the importance of reading aloud, I made a firm commitment to do daily oral reading. I have found the positive results to be worth the time and energy needed to institute this classroom change.

References

Cosgrove, S., & James, R. (1995). *Flutterby.* New York: Price Stern Sloan.
Erickson, J. R. (1991). *Hank the cowdog* (Series). New York: Penguin Group.
Park, B. (1995). *Junie B. Jones* (Series). New York: Random House.
Polacco, P. (1998). *Thank You, Mr. Falker.* New York: Philomel.
Robinson, B. (1982). *The best Christmas pageant ever.* New York: Harper Trophy.

Four-Block Literacy Model: Reaching All Learners

Kathleen Kessel
Dickinson, North Dakota

In classrooms across the country, no matter where you teach, instructing students to read and to become better readers is a primary goal. This goal is a very difficult task because our students enter our classrooms at various reading levels. Most classrooms have students who excel in reading and are at the top of their class, students who struggle and are below grade level, and students who fall somewhere in between. Fortunately, there is a model to teach and improve the reading skills of all students no matter what their reading level, and the model can be used in one classroom without separating students into reading groups. The model is called Four Blocks.

Four Blocks is a framework for reading and writing instruction and was developed by Pat Cunningham, Dottie Hall, and Jim Defee to help all students become successful readers and writers. It was initially used in primary-grade classrooms, but adaptations have been made to provide continued balance for the diverse needs of learners at other grade levels through middle school and beyond.

Teachers use a variety of formats to make each block as multileveled as possible to ensure additional support for students who struggle and additional challenges for students who catch on quickly.

One goal of Four Blocks is to meet individual needs of children without labeling them. Studies prove that this model is successful in improving the reading levels of all students, not just those in the low or average range of ability. In fact, one major research project proved that those children who rank in the top 30% of the performance levels made the greatest gains of all groups.

The Four Blocks model includes four components: guided reading, self-selected reading, writing, and working with words. This instructional model is based on the premise that there are four basic ways children learn to read. The use of this model ensures that all students are exposed to all four methods every day, helping to address individual learning styles and personalities of children at different reading levels within a heterogeneous classroom setting.

In the lower grades, during the guided reading block, approximately three days are spent on grade-level text, and the next two days are spent on below-grade-level text. Teachers teach and model reading strategies through various activities and lessons. In the independent reading block, students read books and materials that are at their grade level and conference at least weekly with teachers, who give them one-to-one help and instruction as needed. Students in the working with words block work with high-frequency words and learn parts of big words (i.e., prefixes, roots, and suffixes, which help them figure out word meanings), spelling patterns, and phonics and decoding skills. During the writing block, teachers use mini-lessons and model writing to help students learn skills such as grammar, usage, punctuation, parts of speech, and cause and effect. Students then spend time on self-selected writing to apply what they have learned.

Planning for Differentiated Instruction at the High School Level

Renee A. Moore
Shelby, Mississippi

For more than nine years, I have conducted ongoing classroom research about teaching Standard English to African American students. That research led me to this belief: Empowering language arts instruction is a dynamic practice. It is shaped by informed and collaborative analysis of the particular cultural experiences, strengths, and learning goals of a specific group of students within a particular community. I refer to this type of teaching practice as culturally engaged instruction (CEI).

One method I use is the personal English plan (PEP). The PEP is an individualized learning plan that I develop with each student in my high school English classes. We start the school year with about two weeks of preassessments, during which I help students gauge their abilities in reading, writing, language mechanics and usage, public speaking, and listening. We analyze this information together to develop a profile.

Next, I present a list of specific learning goals or objectives that I feel are the minimum for successful completion of the course according to state guidelines and my own requirements. Then, in individual conferences, we agree on the specific goals for each student and how these goals will be assessed. Throughout this process, there is much reading and talking about goals, success, and planning.

The students are responsible for their monitoring progress on the PEP. However, I also ask each student to select one significant adult to act as a mentor for the school year. I contact all the mentors and explain that their role is to support and encourage the students to complete their goals. At the end of each nine-week grading period, I meet with each student again as we go over portfolios to determine whether the goals have been met and to what extent. The mentors are invited to attend these meetings if possible. This is how we determine the students' final grade.

Helpful Tips

■ This type of planning can be overwhelming at first, especially if you are teaching six or seven classes a day. The first school year, I only developed plans with one class, until I worked out the logistics.

■ Having students work in reading and writing workshops facilitates the individual planning conferences.

■ Be open-minded in developing the goals. Don't limit the students to adopting goals from the list of state objectives but help them set realistic timelines.

Here are examples of the forms I created to use with students as we develop and evaluate their PEPs.

(Continued)

Renee Moore, NBCT

Student Name _____   Period _____

	Pretest Results	Goals			
		First Nine Weeks	*Second Nine Weeks*	*Third Nine Weeks*	*Fourth Nine Weeks*
Reading					
Writing					
Grammar					
Speaking					
Listening					
Other					

Notes/Comments:

English III/Mrs. R. Moore *Nine Weeks' Evaluation* Verify mentor/parent name, address, phone in index card file.	
1.	What percentage of the total number of tasks has the student completed? _____ number of tasks _____ number completed

2.	Quality of the work
	    a. Average of all scores:_____
	    b. Descriptive comments (special conditions, circumstances that may have affected performance):
	
	 _____
	
	 _____

3.	Mississippi Curriculum Framework
	    a. Number of objectives taught this grading period = _____
	       number passed = _____
	    b. Percentage of objectives taught that student has passed = _____

4.	Adjustments to the PEP
	    a. Addition of personal learning goals
	    b. Deletion or reduction of items
	    c. Adjustment of timeline
	    d. Specific goals for next grading period

5.	Growth Assessment
	    a. *Teacher evaluation of student work.* Attach descriptive comments on student abilities, strengths, and needs
	    b. *Student self-evaluation.* Descriptive comments on student abilities, strengths, and needs (use back or additional sheets as needed)
	      1. What have I learned in English III this nine weeks?
	      2. What do I know or do well? How do I know?
	      3. What do I need to improve or want to learn?
	      4. What would help me to learn or perform better?
	    c. *Mentor's comments.* Made by ___ phone ___ personal visit ___ letter

	Nine weeks' examination grade = average of items 1, 2, and 3. Items 4 and 5 must be completed before grade is recorded.

Student Signature _____ Date _____

Teacher Signature _____ Date _____

Mentor Signature _____ Date _____

CHAPTER 2

Math Techniques to Reach Students

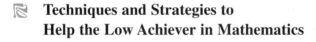 **Techniques and Strategies to Help the Low Achiever in Mathematics**

Curt Boddie
Manhasset, New York

Many students in my twelfth-year college algebra course have experienced some difficulty with mathematics because of one or more of the following reasons:

1. Poor or no organizational skills

2. Intermittent absences, which eliminate the sense of continuity necessary for understanding

3. A lack of diagnostic and prescriptive intervention in earlier years

4. Mathematics material presented in a modality that did not address their learning style

5. Very little experience with success in the discipline

At the beginning of the second full week of school, I give a diagnostic test, requiring the use of paper, pencil, and a calculator. The test assesses simple problem solving, is noncurricular, and is designed to assist me in establishing cooperative learning groups. Based on the results, I form groups of four to five students, making sure each group has a range of strengths. All work completed cooperatively is typically followed, though not always immediately, by an individual assessment addressing the same material that was on the cooperative assignment. This assessment ensures personal accountability. The student who does not manage to perform on the individual assessment at a rate equal to or greater than 75% of the group performance level, loses a favorable group grade.

After the students seem comfortable with the classroom environment and each other, I ask each to pair off with someone, exchange telephone numbers or e-mail addresses, and keep one another informed about class work in case of an absence. The student who is present takes an extra worksheet and gives it to the absent student when he or she returns to class, if not sooner. I do not ask students to deliver materials to other students' homes unless it is convenient and safe to do so. Having students help deliver work to each other raises the sense of responsibility for all students in the class.

At the end of the first unit, each student is asked to do a self-evaluation, truthfully responding to a series of brief but telling statements:

1. I consulted my notes as I did the assigned homework.

2. I attended the math learning center before and after the test.

3. I experienced difficulty doing the math homework.

4. I discussed the unit material with a classmate.

Students can respond *all of the time, some of the time, seldom, rarely,* or *not at all.* They then record which topic or skills areas in the unit gave them the most difficulty and how they intend to address that difficulty in the future.

I also ask that in a separate and anonymous submission they evaluate the unit test. Students comment on whether the test contained only material that was covered in class or on homework assignments, whether there was sufficient space for showing their solution to a given problem, and whether time was a factor in their completion of the test or their performance. Though many students in the course have an IEP that requires the teacher to provide test modifications, the majority of the other students still find time to be a significant factor in how well they perform. I make it a point to give most unit tests over a period of two days, with the bulk of the material tested presented on the first of the two consecutive days of testing.

These four strategies—cooperative learning groups with diverse ability levels, pairing students to share responsibility for informing each other of the classroom activities, self-evaluation at the end of each unit, and assessment designed to diminish time pressures—have served me well in this course, and my immediate supervisor commented favorably on what he observed in the students' academic and attitudinal responses.

▧   Convincing Mathphobics That They Can Be Successful in Math

Cynthia Baird and Jennifer Rhawn
Nokesville, Virginia

Recently, our state instituted a requirement that all high school students must pass an end-of-course statewide test in Algebra I and a test in geometry to graduate. Believing this would pose a challenge to our lower level mathematics students, our district attempted to solve this problem by simply spreading the two curricula over three courses. The distribution of the objectives, however, was left to the individual high schools. Faced with this task, our school's math department agreed to collaboratively analyze the situation as it applied to our students and develop a feasible solution.

As a team, our dialogue centered on why certain students were not successful in the standard algebra–geometry sequence. Our focus was not directed at the slow learner but rather the average student whose potential remained untapped. The consensus was that many students feared math, believing they could never experience success. We surmised that these mathphobics were capable of learning mathematics, but the traditional Algebra I classroom did not mesh with their learning styles. Not encouraged to understand concepts, they merely tried to memorize and repeat teacher-provided algorithms.

Abandoning our established instructional methods and focus would not only be difficult but also imperative. As teachers, we did not want to reteach the same material that had built a conceptual barrier for these students in middle school. Our goal was for students to learn algebra without getting bogged down by poor arithmetic skills. We also felt that we needed to provide these students with techniques to conceptualize algebra before we asked them to solve typical algebra problems. To address multiple learning styles, we strived to incorporate technology and manipulatives whenever applicable. We sought a balance between a structured class environment and a variety of teaching techniques to engage and reach our mathphobics. We would change students' preconceptions about math class from the moment they entered the classroom.

The typical freshman mathematics class begins with a review of everything the students should have learned in middle school but did not. Our math department wanted to set the tone for change from the first day of school. The students had to recognize that they were not simply repeating the same topics they had failed to grasp in the past. We chose to start the course with the concepts involving functions, both because they were easily visualized and because so much of the next four years depended on a strong foundation of functions. We decided that, using temperature and motion detectors, the students would get through the first few classes without calculating a single number. Yet they would walk away with a solid understanding of what a graph represents. Students' negative preconceptions that success in mathematics depends on completing processes rather than understanding them would be shattered.

Designing an impressionable first unit would not be enough to sustain a three-year program. As a department, we knew the importance of long-term planning and decided to plan the full sequence of courses before we began. In choosing the teaching order of the objectives, we considered multiple facets. To sustain student motivation, we interspersed what we felt were the most challenging topics with those the students would find easier. To encourage continual success, we also balanced the objectives—units relying more heavily on direct instruction would be followed by those incorporating manipulatives to teach hands-on, concrete concepts. In addition, we incorporated units involving technology throughout the three-year continuum.

Once we had established the scope and sequence for the courses, our direction turned to the daily classroom environment. We felt that for the students to truly succeed, they had to become more responsible for their own learning. We saw our teaching role as that of a coach, providing students with the necessary equipment and training. By fostering peer dialogue, writing for understanding, and discovery-based activities, we encouraged students to actively develop their conceptual understanding. By engaging in cooperative learning groups, students realized that by helping each other they helped themselves. Creating a classroom community, we led students to take more academic risks— asking questions and offering their opinions in class. Quarterly portfolios required self-reflection as students analyzed their work habits and understanding. They benefited by setting new goals with the awareness of their past pitfalls and successes. From the outset of their high school experience, students became more autonomous learners.

Perhaps the most dramatic realization for these students was that their math teachers expected them to be successful, which until now they had never expected of themselves. All the while they recognized that we had not watered down their curriculum. The three courses were more rigorous than any other math courses the students had taken. They were expected to remain on task for the entire hour-and-a-half class period. The purpose of group work was not to divide up an assignment or activity but rather to collaborate. As teachers, we expected all students to participate in class activities, not just the most confident ones. Nightly homework was assigned with the anticipation of its completion for understanding. We set high expectations from the beginning. When the students rose to meet the challenge, they experienced the pride of earning their success.

The external measure of the program's success came at the end of the second year with the state Algebra I test. What was supposed to be our lowest track class outperformed the district and state averages of traditionally taught Algebra I classes. The following year, the same held true when the students excelled on the geometry state test. The results validated our strategies. By thoroughly and collaboratively analyzing the problem situation, our math department defined a new course sequence. Thoughtful reorganization of the objectives incorporated with the varied techniques to teach them established a new classroom environment. In all, we reached the paramount goal of changing student expectations.

▧ Empowering Students to Accept Challenges

Wesley Yuu
Mililani, Hawaii

In a heterogeneous classroom, creating tasks to meet the needs of all learners can be difficult. Students in the gifted and talented program need to be challenged, but at the same time the task must not overwhelm learners with special needs. Therefore, when I assign a project to my students, I provide them with choices and give them a chance to determine the level at which they want to work.

One of my favorite projects comes at the end of the unit, Samples and Populations (Connected Mathematics project). After students learn how to use box-and-whiskers plots and scatter plots to analyze data, they apply these skills to complete their projects. Every student is given the same scenario:

> You are a biologist working for the Red Cross. In most areas of the United States, tap water is safe to drink and purified drinking water is sold in grocery stores. In many countries, however, people do not have access to safe drinking water. A chart is provided to give you data on the life expectancy and the percentage of people with access to safe drinking water for different countries of the world. Your assignment is to prepare a report that summarizes the relationship between life expectancy and access to safe drinking water. Your report could determine future actions set by the Red Cross.

My class contains students with a range of talents and needs, so I create options to satisfy all levels of learners. Students who are gifted and the high achievers receive the following instructions:

■ The final product must be prepared in a neat, professional manner (as if you are presenting it to the president of a large company).

■ You must provide detailed evidence in a written report, including plots, to back up your conclusion.

- You must prepare a presentation with a visual aid, such as a display board, video, PowerPoint presentation, or any other creative means.

- You may work together if you choose.

Students with special needs are given a booklet that outlines the steps they need to follow to complete the report. Each page contains a different task, such as calculating the five-number summary for the life expectancy in African countries. When they complete the booklet, the students have met the goal of the project and earn a maximum grade of 85%. They are then given the option of preparing a presentation that can earn them 15 additional points. While most of my students with special needs are satisfied with simply completing the booklet, some see the presentation as a challenge and give it a try. They see what the gifted students are doing and borrow some of their ideas when making their own display boards. This, I believe, is one of the strengths of having a heterogeneous class.

For the average learner, a simple outline is provided, which serves as a checklist. Whereas the special needs booklet provides detailed worksheets for each minitask, the outline simply lists what needs to be done. The students check off each item as it is completed. When their report is complete, they, too, are given the same option to make a presentation.

Student expectations vary depending on the learner, but the products are assessed using the same rubric: The box-and-whiskers plots and scatter plots must accurately represent the data, the products have to be neat, and the conclusions have to be sufficiently justified. Even though students with special needs receive extra assistance with the booklets, their reports still need to be prepared in a professional manner, and their calculations need to be accurate.

I have assigned this project for the past three years, and I am always amazed at the results. Although the presentations are not required of average students or those with special needs, most make the decision to strive for the maximum possible points. Next year, I plan to add another component for my gifted students. They will complete an inquiry-based research project to further study other factors in countries around the world that affect life expectancy. I bet that if I make this optional for my other students, they, too, will rise to the challenge.

CHAPTER 3

Teaching With Technology

 Technology and ADHD

Helen F. Melvin
Frenchville, Maine

Steven blew into my second-grade class on the first day of school, like a whirlwind. He was the most hyperactive student I'd ever seen. Whenever he walked around the classroom, he knocked things down; he could not manage to remain still. Though bright, Steven had a hard time focusing, and his work suffered. Support for schoolwork at home was very limited.

The first week of school, I prioritized what I wanted to change immediately. The most annoying behavior was the constant noise. I employed a behavior plan, which dealt with the noise problem. The noise started to diminish and eventually totally stopped. The first few days I gave him fifteen chances a day, and I talked with him often. The chances diminished as the noises decreased. Eventually, noises were no longer an issue. Steven had a problem with his writing skills. He didn't like any type of writing. He did not like to write and would write only one or two words on his paper, while other students wrote complete stories.

My classroom has sixteen computers, allowing each student to have his or her own. I started a unit on local history and genealogy using technology. One of the assignments was for students to bring home a digital camera and take pictures of their family and surroundings. I then downloaded the pictures at school. Students and parents were always anxious to view the results; however, pictures could not be printed unless students wrote an accompanying story. One weekend Steven borrowed the camera and took pictures of his grandmother and grandfather, and I downloaded the pictures at school. He was very anxious to have them printed, so he could show his grandmother. After I downloaded his pictures and Steven viewed them on the computer, he wanted some copies, so he started writing. Steven wrote stories during his spare time and asked to stay in during recess or before school to get printouts of his pictures. His writing improved by leaps and bounds. By the end of second grade, Steven was on par with the other students.

Technology can be a great way to motivate students. Students with attention deficit hyperactivity disorder (ADHD) are generally not hyperactive at a computer, and most can focus for long periods of time when using a computer. Writing by using technology tools changed Steven. The computer also removed his fear of failure. It's easier to take risks with a computer than to fail among one's peers. For Steven, the computer helped him develop skills that he wouldn't have achieved otherwise.

Technology and Shyness

Helen F. Melvin
Frenchville, Maine

Justin was one of the shyest second graders I had ever encountered. His answers to classroom questions were mere whispers. Where other students couldn't wait to share their written stories on the Author's Chair, Justin refused to read them aloud. Instead, he asked me to read his work. This continued for four months.

In January I decided to show the students how to use the PowerPoint program to present research on local history. Justin and his friend, Randy, chose to present research on deer their fathers hunted. They brought digital cameras home, and each student took pictures of his father's deer (caught during hunting season). Then they incorporated these pictures into their PowerPoint presentations. Both boys worked diligently to prepare their joint report. After completing the writing portion of their presentations, students practiced presenting their research in class. Justin and Randy had no problem presenting their PowerPoint presentation on the classroom screen. They took turns explaining and embellishing their report pages. Later we invited parents to view the students' presentations. Once again, Justin was a dynamic instructor as he presented his report to all assembled, the soft voice now replaced with an audible voice. For the rest of the school year, Justin did his own readings and presentations. PowerPoint truly brought him out of his shell and into the limelight.

Using Technology to Reach At-Risk Students

Laurie Richards
Brewer, Maine

Brian is a first-grade student in my class. He is very small for his age. His kindergarten teacher repeatedly told me to keep an eye on him and watch for signs of abuse. He was referred to our Reading Recovery teachers from the kindergarten school for possible extra help with reading; the Reading Recovery teachers were to check his progress early in the year. My principal told me that Brian is just a typical attention deficit disorder (ADD) kid. Nobody really seemed to know Brian.

At the beginning of the school year, Brian was very shy and reserved. He was frequently tardy or absent. Brian did not talk and did not participate in class discussions. He did not volunteer. When asked a question, Brian would not respond. When given work to do, Brian would just sit there and wait for me to come to him. He would do his work as long as I stood there with him, but the minute I left he was daydreaming. Nothing seemed to excite Brian. I began to worry about him.

I kept a close eye on Brian. I did not see the signs of abuse that his kindergarten teacher told me about, but I could see that if I did not reach him soon, he was going to fall through the cracks. I talked with his parents. Nothing changed. In his first semester report card, I wrote of my concerns to his parents. His behaviors still didn't change. I tried to give Brian special jobs to bring him out, and I still couldn't reach him.

In October I was awarded an Internet Innovator award from National Semiconductor. The award was for a project that I had done with my students the previous year involving the Internet and technology in the classroom. With this award, the school received money and was able to use part of the award to purchase a laptop computer lab. Before having this lab, each classroom had only one computer with Internet access. With about twenty children in each class, it was difficult to find time for all children to have access to the computer.

After the Christmas break, our school acquired the new lab with sixteen computers, a laser printer, and hardware for wireless networking. We now have a larger ratio of computers to students, which allows more children to use the computers, and they also have more computer time. I try to use technology as a tool for learning whenever I can in the classroom. The lab is stored in my classroom, so the children helped me get everything unpacked and running. The school purchased software for the computers, and I had my first graders help me load it onto the machines. They were so excited about these new computers, and they took them very seriously. The children were then introduced to the proper care and handling of the computers.

I then introduced the children to the word processing program on the computers and encouraged anyone who wanted to use the computers for writing workshop—rather than using paper and pencil—to do so. Brian chose the computer. It wasn't that he couldn't use paper and pencil; he could. I started to see small changes in Brian. He asked me if he could use the laptop when he finished his work. I allowed him to do so, and his face lit up. Brian started to raise his hand to ask me questions about the laptop, and I helped him out. I could see his confidence coming through, and I knew that I had to act fast to keep his confidence growing. I began to ask Brian to help others with computer tasks, such as opening programs, quitting programs, and shutting down the computers.

We began a theme on weather, which started with the four seasons. Using the computers and a program called Kid Pix Studio Deluxe, I had the children create slideshows depicting the four seasons. The children created five slides: a cover slide and a slide for each season. They added music and sound effects to their shows. I observed Brian as he learned how to record his own voice for the slideshow to name each season. Before long he had children gathered around him to learn how they could add sound to their own slide shows. Brian had changed from a child who didn't talk in the back of the room to a child who was the center of everyone's attention.

Brian started to shine. He began to raise his hand in class. He would sit down and get his work done, knowing that when he finished he could use the computers. He asked for help when he needed it. It was happening! Not only was Brian participating in class and asking for help when he needed it, but he had discovered something that he was good at and could help others with.

Brian went from a nonreader to an average first-grade reader in a matter of a few weeks. He didn't qualify for Reading Recovery help, is a regular participant in class, and has fewer tardies and absences. He gets his work done on time. Brian has mastered our district's technology benchmarks through the fourth-grade level. Brian is shining. By using a computer as a learning tool, Brian was saved before he could fall through the cracks.

Helpful Tips

■ Start slow. I began by first instructing children in the proper way to take the computers out of the cart, carry them, turn them on and off, and put them away.

■ Have your first lesson on the computers be something that you do step-by-step with the class.

■ Don't be afraid to let the children explore. They may just teach you something.

CHAPTER **4**

Teaching Techniques

 Reaching a Child With Asperger Syndrome

Cynthia L. Pochomis
Wilmington, Delaware

The question that had perplexed me since Steven was assigned to my self-contained special education class one October had been, "Why won't this intelligent, creative, and passionate young man write his thoughts and responses?" Steven could orally respond to any question, he engaged in lively and appropriate discussion, and he answered one-word or short-answer assessments correctly. Yet when it came to composition, a response to literature, or an explanation of a problem, Steven did not write.

To answer this question, I had to first determine if there was a physical problem that prevented Steven from writing. To make sure Steven was capable of writing, I enlisted the help of an occupational therapist and a speech-language therapist. After extensive testing, both concluded that there was no physical reason for Steven's inability to write.

This result led me to believe that the cause for Steven's problems in writing was behavioral. I consulted with Steven's mother. She had placed Steven in six different schools, even moving to change districts, looking for the best educational setting for Steven. He was not successful in any of the prior placements and had been hospitalized twice for suicidal threats. She said that he was distressed about people's responses to him but did not seem to understand how his behavior affected others. He had been on three different medications to address depression, mood stability, and attention deficit hyperactivity disorder (ADHD). She believed that the medications aggravated rather than relieved Steven's symptoms, so, under the doctor's supervision, she discontinued them before he was placed in my class. She informed me that, after many different diagnoses, Steven's psychiatrist and medical team members told her that Steven had Asperger syndrome.

A child with this syndrome may have normal intelligence and language development but may also exhibit autistic-like behaviors and marked deficiencies in social and communication skills. Children with Asperger syndrome have difficulty reading nonverbal cues and determining proper body space. They may be overly sensitive to sounds, tastes, smells, or textures and appear eccentric or odd. Their language development may be extraordinarily rich, or they may be extremely literal and have difficulty using language in a social context. Writing may prove difficult. Steven's mother shared a wealth of information with me about this syndrome. After reading the information, we sat down together to make a consistent plan for changing Steven's inappropriate behaviors and improving his academic and social skills. We wanted to set reasonable expectations that would be consistent both at home and at school.

In the classroom, I emphasized turn taking, listening skills, complimenting, responding, joining others, and accepting the answers and successes of others. Because Steven took so many things literally, I also tried to joke with him and to use plays on words along with similes and metaphors, followed by explanations of their meanings. I enlisted the help of a popular male paraprofessional to include Steven in his daily team sports at recess. At first, Steven balked at this type of activity, but he soon realized that playing an organized game could be fun, even if he wasn't the best at it.

As long as Steven was engaged in a high-interest activity, his classroom behavior was acceptable. If asked to perform a task that did not interest him, he became disruptive. He made noises, put things in his mouth, played with his supplies, and disturbed those around him. If corrected, Steven denied any wrongdoing on his part. After finding activities that Steven considered to be rewarding, I initiated a point system to help shape his behavior. Points were awarded for increments of time on task. These started small and were gradually lengthened. Because every child deserves a safe leaning environment, I first targeted the behaviors that threatened the other students' well-being—acts of physical aggression, insults, and noise making. Once these were under control, I worked with Steven on acceptable use of classroom materials, task completion, peer relations, and self-stimulation.

Placing Steven in my class was his mother's last attempt at including him in public education. His mother and doctors had started the paperwork for a rare and complex placement, which would place Steven in a private, boarding school-type of facility not available in our state. However, the minute he walked in the door, I began to shape his behavior so that he could remain in the public school system. He was already learning. In spite of his failures, he knew more than most children his age and should have qualified for a gifted program. My classroom and approach to instruction were not like any that Steven had encountered. I emphasize kindness and respect above all other things.

I am also a little like Miss Frizzle of *Magic School Bus* fame. Thanks to my grant-writing ability and the generosity of local businesses, my room has a complete kitchen; more than 1,000 trade books; a lizard, birds, turtles, snakes, various insects (including butterflies and hissing cockroaches), hamsters, and fish. I have two successful classroom businesses—Kidwormco, a profitable worm company; and a class bakery. The children are involved in all decisions regarding the money they make. This makes the learning that accompanies these ventures more meaningful to the students and provides life-skills training. When Steven came into the class, we were involved in a successful statewide adoption of the tiger swallowtail as our state butterfly. Steven was fascinated by everything and eager to become involved. This made it possible for me to implement my behavior modification plan. Steven earned his way into involvement with the plants, animals, connecting blocks, and cooking tasks as a reward for proper behavior.

My plan to improve Steven's behavior was overwhelmingly successful. His mother stated that this was the happiest she and Steven had ever been. They were also more relaxed because she was not constantly being called to school for his unacceptable behavior. She even spent several days volunteering, lending her artistic talents to our class.

Once Steven's behavior was manageable, my focus shifted to his academic potential. I tried to design instruction that was meaningful for Steven, based on what I had learned about his interests and the way in which Asperger syndrome affected his learning style. For independent study, I allowed Steven to choose from the many topics that held his interest. I would pose a problem and let him find the solution using the resources available in the room. He was free to choose the novels he read from a selection I had available. He had a Web page, which he updated monthly, called "Steven's Amazing Insects." He searched out the most interesting facts about insects and worked with the technology teacher to post them on the school's Web site. Since he refused to touch the worms for packaging and delivery, I put him in charge of book-keeping for the company. He kept our finances up-to-date.

Steven needed to learn to function as part of a group. I made myself a checklist that I felt would help me in planning lessons for Steven when he was part of group instruction. I used it to remind me of the strategies that worked successfully with Steven and shared it with others who were teaching him. I talked with Steven to try to discover those things that were most distracting to him and that caused him to be disruptive. I learned to give him more space around his desk, to ask the other children not to stare at him, and to pair him with selected individuals. I also read many current articles on Asperger syndrome and contacted one of my former university professors for current findings in the area.

I noticed that if Steven turned to a page in a textbook or workbook with a large number of problems or questions, he shut down and reverted to inappropriate behavior. Instead of rewriting the books or exercises I used in my instruction, I had Steven make several blocking devices. These devices consisted of black construction paper with a different size hole cut from each piece. Steven cut the holes and lami-nated the pieces. This process fascinated him and he offered to make the devices for others in the class who wanted to try them. Steven placed the appropriately sized piece of paper with the window over the problem on which he was currently working. This allowed him to block out the rest of the information on the page and concentrate on one problem at a time. Instead of completing an entire set of exercises, Steven chose a sampling of problems that demonstrated his mastery of a concept.

Progress in writing was very slow. Steven typed using the hunt-and-peck method, so keyboarding was not an option yet. I purchased a touch-typing program that Steven used daily to increase his rate and accuracy.

Using my checklist, I tried to design Steven's writing assignments to be meaningful. I broke each down into small components and then put them together to make a whole that was appropriate for his ability level. I told Steven that he must write to show the rest of us how much he knows. In October I gave him a journal and asked him to write only one thought each day. If he got stumped, I gave him some choices of words or phrases to get him started. By November, I expected two sentences and by December, three. He succeeded with this initial step. At my urging, his mother bought him a diary with a lock and asked him to write something in it each day. Of course, we never read this. As an alternative means of assessment I also had Steven record some of his answers to questions if a longer response was required. He enjoyed working with the tape recorder and produced some excellent work this way.

When I first learned that Steven was coming to my classroom, I panicked. His file was full of horrifying behavioral incidents that included acts of aggression against fellow students and an assault on a paraprofessional. He had stabbed her through the hand with a pencil. I spent most of September molding and shaping the behavior of students in my class, and we were beginning to function as a unit. New students always upset the dynamics until their niche is found. In Steven's case, it was more like upheaval. At first Steven's mother was very wary of another teacher dealing with her son. They had only known failure in the school system. It took a lot of effort to bring her around to working collaboratively for Steven's welfare.

It turns out that working with Steven and his mother was one of the most rewarding experiences of my long teaching career. Steven is an intelligent and complex boy. I watched his behavior develop from acting like a wounded animal to becoming a confident and successful young man.

It was necessary for me to change my teaching style to accommodate Steven's needs. I gave him the space he required, shortened assignments, explained jokes and nuances of language, and learned more about using technology for instruction. I collaborated with Steven's mother and made connections with professionals who were familiar with Asperger syndrome. I included alternatives to writing by using videotaped or audiotaped responses. Letter writing as a means of obtaining desired results and an Internet pen pal for keyboarding and communication practice increased the amount and variety of Steven's writing. Returning him to the mainstream became a realistic goal. I honestly believe that someday I will read about Steven as an inventor, researcher, or entomologist. He already possesses the skills; he just needed someone to help him learn to use them effectively.

Helpful Tips

Teaching Tips for Reaching Students With Asperger Syndrome

1. Learn all that you can about the syndrome.

2. Collaborate with other professionals. Contact your local university professors for more information and assistance.

3. View parents as partners and collaborators for your student's welfare. They can provide a wealth of information.

4. Talk with your student. Find out what interests him or her and use that knowledge to develop meaningful assignments.

5. Shorten assignments.

6. Explain jokes and nuances of language.

7. Give your student the space he or she needs.

8. Model, teach, and reward acceptable behavior.

9. Use technology as a compensatory tool.

10. Keep your sense of humor.

▨   For Autism, Consistency Is Essential

Linda Hickam
Olathe, Kansas

Autism was a diagnosis that a character in a movie was living with and that his family was learning would impact their daily lives—autism was not something I had in my classroom or something I had given much thought to until seven years ago. I was told in April of that year that the following August I would have Ryan, a student with autism, as a full inclusion student in my fourth-grade classroom. I began to seek out the people and the information I would need to make the next year successful for all of us—Ryan, the other students, and myself.

I began gathering articles explaining best practices for children with autism. I talked to people who had worked with Ryan, and they also gave me information that would help me prepare for the coming school year. I spent the summer reading articles and searching the Internet for any information I could find that might be helpful. I went to visit Ryan's parents and watched videos of him as a young child playing with a litter of new puppies before he was diagnosed with autism. What I found difficult was that I could have been watching my own children at age two years, playing, talking, and laughing. How Ryan communicated now was a world away from the little boy in the video, and I could understand the frustration his parents were experiencing, trying to find the best course to take for Ryan's education and future. I thought I had done all that I could to prepare for the year, but what I had in my mind was not exactly what Ryan had in his.

Ryan's sister brought him to our classroom every morning. She was a previous student of mine and was always very helpful and insightful about how Ryan was feeling that day. To make days successful for Ryan, we had to have consistency, routine, and structure. We created picture icons that could be adhered to a strip of paper on Ryan's desk that would visually represent, for Ryan, that particular school day. The icons were crucial because any change in the schedule was difficult for Ryan. The night before each school day, I organized the following day's schedule.

We also implemented a reward system for Ryan. In the morning when Ryan arrived, we asked him what he wanted for a reward that day. He had a list of several activities from which he could choose. The activities could be as simple as getting to sit in the rocking chair and read a book about the *Titanic*—Ryan's favorite book. Ryan had a strip of laminated construction paper to which pennies could be adhered. After earning the specified number of pennies, Ryan attained his reward. Pennies were earned by completing work and demonstrating appropriate behavior. It was important that Ryan knew before beginning a task what the expectations were for the lesson and behavior. I learned very quickly that consistency was key to Ryan's success.

The other students in the class that year were amazing. Most of the students had known Ryan for years, but I still asked one of the adults who worked with Ryan to visit the class to talk about autism, and I made sure to do this when Ryan was not present. The students worked with Ryan on a rotating schedule. They worked with him in class, they worked with him at recess, they worked with him at home, and they worked with him on weekends. Ryan developed an incredible rapport with the students.

During that school year I learned more about autism than I could have learned in a summer of reading articles. I learned that children with autism need a program that is individualized to meet their specific needs. I learned that modification of the curriculum and expectations was ongoing and constantly changing. I also learned that consistency is essential for all children—with or without special needs—to be successful in the classroom.

Seven years ago I had my first experiences with a child with autism. I have had at least one child with autism in my classroom every year since then. I have since moved from fourth grade to sixth grade, so I have had some of these children twice. I have learned a great deal from these children and their families. They have shown me how different autism is in each child. I am not sure who taught more during these past few years, the students or me. I do know that each child has enriched my life and made me see the potential that each individual child has to be successful.

Helpful Tips

1. Establish and consistently follow a schedule.

2. Develop a rapport with the parents and any adult who works with the child. You will need their help to make the year successful.

3. Make sure everyone understands the student with autism is in the classroom to learn and be sure to include him or her in all activities.

4. Modify curriculum and expectations and modify some more.

5. Do not have rigid expectations. Every child with autism is different, and what worked for one may not, and probably won't, work for another.

6. Enjoy the diversity that having a child with autism in the classroom gives.

Magic Happens Here

Jeannette Lucey, IHM Sister
Philadelphia, Pennsylvania

When first beginning to teach in this inner city school eighteen years ago, I realized that the only thing thought cool or celebrated was sports. Believing in the potential of the children and wanting to unlock the treasures within, I took on the role of contest coordinator and began to watch for and enter them in every competition possible. The results have been astounding: first place two years in a row and various other places in National History Day; ten-year winners in various speech tournaments (individual and team trophies); State Geography and Math champs; essay and art winners; academic scholarships; published poetry and television, newspaper, and radio interviews with children; science and environmental awards; and the list goes on. The outcome is 500 or more children each year who believe in themselves, who walk with pride, who carry themselves with dignity, who have self-esteem and a willingness to attempt anything, and who are convinced that they and the school are number one. We discovered and exposed a multitude of talents that went beyond the textbook and pencils, and we now celebrate everything.

Some children have written about our school, saying that magic happens here. It may seem so, but we are aware that magicians practice long and hard to make magic look easy. The results are most rewarding. It's not magic, but it's been a magical experience for our children. The contest coordinator has been the catalyst.

Our school zip code neighborhood is listed as having the second highest homicide rate in the city of Philadelphia. Many of the children I teach have had parents, siblings, relatives, friends, or neighbors killed or wounded in drive-by shootings. Violence enters the classroom in numerous ways: Rumors, gossip, put downs, and use of force or weapons to solve conflicts are a way of life for many.

Realizing that learning is difficult under these circumstances, I tapped into our school peace program and began sending students to the Peace Room when they want to fight. There they sit face to face and have no need to keep up a tough facade for the benefit of onlookers. This room has a round table with a painting of the biblical lion and lamb (unlikely friends able to live together). The room is painted in bright, cheerful colors and is decorated with artifacts from the more than thirty countries from which our children come. There is an apparent calm present, which usually enables the students to come to some kind of settlement. (They tell us it isn't always easy, and sometimes they just agree to disagree.) The only rule is that the one holding the toy lamb (which is always on the table) has the right to speak. This helps a great deal when all want to talk at once.

Periodically when I sense a buildup of tension, conflict, or bullying, I have the students push their chairs to the perimeter of the classroom and make a statement about what I observe as problematic. Students are asked to comment or express their feelings about the situation. They must use names, not just "some kids do or say this." Each and every student in the class is called on to talk, since we are all members of the group and have responsibility for each other. I tell them to face the person they are speaking to or about as they talk. When the bullies or offenders realize that many of their classmates stand against their behaviors, they have, on occasion, apologized and promised to change. I call it a class meeting; another teacher in our school designates it laundry day. The practice has been successful and has greatly relieved tensions. It has proven to be a good tool in sensitizing children who bully about how their actions affect others.

High-End Learners: Providing Support

Stephanie Blackburn
Bradford, Rhode Island

Many classrooms today are filled with a wide range of learners. Typically the abilities in my classroom range from two years below to more than two years above grade level in all academic areas. It is a continual challenge to meet all of those needs. At each level, children need different services and support. The higher end student needs just as much support as the lower end student. If left alone, high-end students often become unmotivated and at times problematic.

"Just wait!" a third-grade teacher said one winter day during lunch. She proceeded to describe a student who would be coming to fourth grade the following year. As she depicted Sue, all the other teachers at the table began to chime in: "Doesn't work to her potential . . . ", "Won't work on her weaknesses . . . ", "Has difficulty working with her peers . . . ", "Others won't take chances when she's around . . . ", "She's a straight-A student but she's got no thirst for knowledge." All I could do was sigh and begin thinking of strategies to address this child who would be in my room in fewer than six months.

I used a technique I learned early in my teaching profession: make connections with students. Even though Sue wasn't in my class yet, she would be soon enough, so I decided to establish a relationship early. From that point on I made it a priority to seek Sue out. I spoke to her in the lunchroom, the bus line, classrooms, anywhere I'd run into her. I talked to her about school-related issues, joked around with her about her friends, and asked her about her family. After a few weeks, she began seeking me out. My comments and questions then focused on academic-related issues. I'd ask her what she was learning and then pose "I wonder why" questions and walk away. Initially she would shrug her shoulders. Then she began responding negatively: "Whatever. Who cares? It doesn't really matter." I didn't want to lose her just yet. The next day I would ask her if she had an answer. When she replied with "no," I provided the answer for her. I always expressed a keen interest in the topic as well. I'd then say, "I wonder if . . ." and begin the cycle all over again. It started becoming a game, and she became hooked. Each day I saw her she'd ask for the answer to the question from the day before. After about a week, I stopped answering the questions. One day she appeared in my classroom, looking for the previous day's answer. "Oh, I don't remember!" I said. "I bet if you went online you'd be able to find it in ten minutes. My computers are open. Why don't I send a note down to your teacher and let her know you are doing me a favor? Then you can find it out for both of us. I am anxious to know myself!" With that she sighed and plopped herself at the computer and began plugging away. Within five minutes she found the answer, ran over to me, and started spouting out the information. She then continued the game, saying, "I wonder if . . ." For the remainder of the year we played the game, but she became the inquirer and the seeker of the knowledge.

The next fall Sue strode into my room. I had some initial plans but still didn't know where she stood academically. The first few weeks of school I administered a number of preassessments as well as an interest inventory with all of the students in my class. I needed to know where each one was, so I could plan for and proceed through my year. As expected, Sue was strong in linguistics but average in math. I would be able to compact her curriculum in reading and language arts, but she'd need to be included in the whole-class math instruction.

After identifying the skills she had mastered, I sat with her to create goals and objectives. What would she be doing? She expressed an interest in writing a piece of historical fiction based on concepts we were exploring as a whole class. We mapped out a plan, and I introduced her to goal setting. From that point she was in charge of her goals (with my approval). Daily she documented her tasks and committed herself to them. If she did not complete the goals she had listed in class, she then had homework. Her mother reported a dramatic increase in her motivation. Sue was reading various articles on the topic she had chosen and borrowing books from the library. I put her in touch with a local historian, who helped her find some primary sources. During the research process I worked with her individually to analyze historical fiction as well as other writing techniques. She needed some instruction on note taking and types of resources. She grasped and applied the concepts quickly. We met constantly to review, plan, and learn together. Although the support I provided was not in the form of skills instruction, which was what the rest of the class was receiving, I did offer help to improve her work. At that time I delivered any direct instruction she needed to be successful.

I had no problem with Sue in a whole-group setting. During whole-class discussions she let others provide input and seemed genuinely interested in them. She debated but learned quickly that her opinion wasn't always fact. The other students no longer feared the wrath of Sue but respected her opinion. There was a transformation in the entire room. Those children who were at one point intimidated by this girl were now listening to her and debating her ideas and comments. As the year proceeded, she submitted her work for formal publication, and she independently entered many other writing contests. Sue had taken charge of her learning. I was truly only the facilitator, not a teacher.

Helpful Tips

- Develop relationships with students as early as possible.
- Identify strengths and needs; concentrate on existing knowledge and work on needs.
- Identify interests and plan activities accordingly.
- Plan goals with the student.
- Make students responsible for their progress and goals.
- Provide contact to other experts in the field as well as other resources.
- Model the learning process and the excitement of it.
- Incorporate high-end activities into the class instruction.

Catching a Student Being Good

Patricia Kammeyer
Antwerp, Ohio

When Petunia entered my classroom, I was immediately struck by her wide-eyed expression, a mixture of mischief and defiance. She sullenly made her way to an empty seat and sat at attention waiting to see what was going to come next. This was the first day of a new school year and for Petunia the seventh school she had attended in just four short years. She knew the drill: sit down, be quiet, and fade into the background; no one will notice you're in the class, and, what's worse, no one will care.

Before the morning was over, Petunia had let down her guard, and her personality began to emerge. She was boisterous, antagonistic, and argumentative. It was apparent that her social skills were far below the rest of the class. I found myself spending what was supposed to be teaching time on discipline. It seems every time I began an activity or project, Petunia found a way to disrupt the class, and I was immediately sucked into telling her all the reasons why her behavior was unacceptable and what my expectations were. As I focused my attention on Petunia, she sat with a smile and behaved. As soon as I would turn my attention to teaching, she would act up.

I went home that first day feeling exhausted and outwitted. I replayed the day's events in my mind and came to a realization. It was suddenly clear to me that when I was correcting Petunia she had my complete attention, which was exactly what she yearned for. Negative attention was for her—a foster child who felt unloved and unaccepted—better than no attention. To reach and change her I would have to give her the attention she sought.

I entered my classroom the next morning with a plan. As soon as Petunia walked through my door, I immediately focused my attention on her and told her what books she needed to get out on her desk to begin the day's lessons. I then complimented her on how quickly she followed my direction and thanked her. As the day proceeded, Petunia disrupted and tried to get me off track. Remembering what I had figured out the previous night, I completely ignored all but the most outrageous interruptions and instead focused my attention on her good behavior. Each time I saw an appropriate classroom behavior, I made it a point to tell her how proud I was of her, how happy I was to have such a hardworking student, and how special she was because she listened and followed class procedures.

Change was slow, but within a few weeks I began to see a little girl who was still starved for attention but who was doing appropriate things to get the attention she craved. As her behavior improved, she began to make friends with the other girls in the class. These friendships helped fill her need for acceptance and attention. Over time, as she could focus her energy on appropriate class behavior, her grades also began to improve.

When the year was over, I was sad to see Petunia leave my class. But I was thankful for the lesson she had taught me. It has served me well in my teaching career.

CHAPTER 5

Science to Reach
All Learners

 The Big Hole River Education Program

Allen R. Bone
Butte, Montana

A teacher from the high school and I (from a middle school) began an after-school program by taking interested students out to collect water data at four sites along a stream that runs through Butte. We were able to use our personal cars for transportation for about four years until, with no advanced notice, we were told district policy prohibited transporting students in personal cars. We needed funding to keep our program going and approached our curriculum director. He knew about the program and wanted us to expand it into the elementary schools. My high school partner also wanted to retire and convinced other teachers from the high school to continue the program.

Our curriculum director provided funding for a team of teachers to attend a SITES (Science Improvement Through Environmental Science) workshop, training teachers at all levels to work together

55

using science. The high school and middle school teachers trained our students to act as mentors for the elementary students, and our SITES program was formed. At our peak we had three high school teachers, one middle school teacher, and three elementary teachers, with all of our classes monitoring watersheds around Butte. This worked for a number of years.

Unfortunately our curriculum director retired, too, and our funding was cut again. We have had several supporting grants over the years for special events. A few years ago ARCO (Atlantic Richfield) paid for teachers to run stations for eight elementary school classes and paid for three middle school teams to come to the river for a couple of days. Montana Fish and Game and Project WET have been very supportive with supplies and substitute costs. Our high school teachers have paid for transportation with their science budgets most years. Through the dedication of two high school teachers and myself we continue to reach out.

Maybe it is our bullheadedness, but we realized the importance of taking students out to the river to collect real data and bringing data back to the classroom for interpretation. The Paul F. Brandwein Institute, the Big Hole River Foundation, and the Toyota Tapestry Project have also realized the importance of student-collected data. Through them, the Big Hole River Education Program was started. We use highly motivated seventh-grade and high school students as student teachers for field trips along the river. Our students instruct elementary students from six rural elementary schools by demonstrating scientific methods, assessment techniques, and ecological concepts.

These experiences give the rural students the opportunity to understand the science behind the water they live on, and they give the city students the opportunity to be teachers for a day. What is the best practice in this? I think it is the dedication of the teachers who believe in themselves and their countless hours of commitment to this program. We see the importance of the project and continue to give of ourselves for the students. Many students benefit from the program: The middle and high school students from Butte serve as mentors and have expanded fieldwork opportunities, rural students and their teachers are introduced to new topics through hands-on activities, and the field trips promote an interest in science and encourage students to get involved in additional science classes and clubs.

Our students enjoy the opportunity to get involved, even knowing ahead of time that they need to come to extra hours of training and make up all of their class assignments missed while on field trips. The students have to perform well in all of their classes. It is an extremely large commitment, even before we step out of the school. They realize that from the beginning and step up to the plate, ready to take on the challenge. The students have a wide range of academic ability. Most are in the upper middle range, some are special needs, and some are gifted. All of them learn good work ethics and raise their grades, usually by two letter grades throughout the year. A poster I have in my classroom sums up what I believe causes the increased grades: "I remember 95% of what I teach!"

Is the program a success? I see brothers and sisters of former students joining my science club. I see former students as well as students from the rural schools taking more science in high school to have this opportunity. Is my time worth it? When I have the opportunity to see a seventh grader hand-in-hand with a kindergartener, who is wearing child-size fishing boots, walking out into the water, radiating excitement, I say, yes, it is worth it; most definitely it is worth it.

 Where Does Your Burger Come From?

Rebecca J. Baker
Hartville, Missouri

Author's Note: The author wishes to acknowledge the Wright County, Missouri, Farm Bureau; Missouri Farm Bureau; and South Carolina Farm Bureau for some of the ideas and information included in this lesson.

Subject Area: Communication Arts,
Math, Science, Health (Nutrition)

Grade levels: 2–3, 4–5; could be modified to include any learning level

Objectives

1. To classify and visualize foods in a burger by origin—plant source or animal source

2. To identify the part of the plant (root, stem, leaf, or flower/seed) in a burger

3. To categorize foods in a burger by food groups

4. To create a burger meal and evaluate it according to the five food groups

5. To assess and explain the cost of a burger given a table of cost per ingredients

Materials and Equipment

Picture, drawing, or model of a burger or a supply of paper, scissors, glue, yarn, and felt to make burger models

Writing paper, pencils, word or picture cards for activities and assessments

Venn diagram or other graphic organizer

Time Required

Forty-five to ninety minutes

Activities and assessments may be divided into different days or time frames to accommodate schedule. The amount of time required will vary depending on grade level and how many of the suggested activities and performance tasks or assessments are used.

Steps a Teacher Needs to Follow to Implement the Lesson

Preparation

Have available to the students an assortment of paper (construction, bond, or tag board) and yarn or felt to be used to create burgers.

Optional: Make a model of a burger (hamburger or cheeseburger) out of fabric, paper, or tag board. Students can draw the components of the burger on the board, poster, or paper as the lesson is presented.

Directions for Making a Three-Dimensional Model

Inside bun: Cut two tan circles of desired size

Outside bun: Cut two darker tan, golden brown circles for the baked crust side

Hamburger: Cut brown circle for the burger

Cheese: Cut yellow square for American, light yellow or off-white with holes for Swiss, and so on

Tomato: Cut red circle

Onion: Cut white circle and long white strips (or use white yarn)

Diced onion: Cut small pieces of paper or yarn

Pickles: Cut small circles of green

Ketchup: Cut strips of red paper or yarn

Mustard: Cut dark yellow strips of paper or yarn

Mayonnaise: Cut white strips

Lettuce: For shredded lettuce, use green paper that has been shredded in a paper shredder; for leaf lettuce, cut fanlike shapes of green paper

Sesame seeds: Use real sesame seeds

For a fabric model of a burger, cut pieces as suggested with these exceptions: The outside bun pieces should be ½ to 1 in. (depends on the overall size desired) larger than the inside pieces so that when they are sewn together they will make pillows. Use embroidered French knots for sesame seeds if desired.

Also, for the hamburger and tomato, cut two pieces of dark brown and red fabric. Add a couple of layers of quilt batting before they are sewn together. Add grill marks to the brown hamburger with a marker or fabric paints. Use dark pink felt to add a seedy area to red tomato. Use felt or heavy fabric for the other components as suggested for paper.

Word cards can be made and used as vocabulary cards and with the graphic organizer activities. Picture cards can be used with younger students.

Lesson

If you have a paper or fabric model of a burger available, pass out the components or pieces of the burger to the students. Starting with the bun, each student tells about his or her component and uses the component to build a burger model. The other students and the teacher then add more information as needed. The lesson could include the following information:

Bun. Bread is the world's most widely eaten food. It is made from flour. Flour comes from the kernels or seeds of wheat and other grains (oats, rye, barley, soybeans, corn, millet, rice, etc.). Wheat is the most common grain grown in the United States. The kernels or seeds are harvested in the spring or summer by a machine called a combine and taken to a mill and ground into flour. The flour is then made into buns at a bakery. Buns are in the grain food group, also called breads and cereals food group, and supply carbohydrates for the body. Carbohydrates give us energy.

Sesame seeds. Seeds of the sesame plant may be on the bun. The seeds add flavor, protein, vitamins, and minerals. Sesame seeds are especially high in calcium and phosphorus, which help build strong bones and teeth. However, the amount on a hamburger bun is so small it will not add significantly to a person's daily nutritional intake.

Hamburger. The meat of the hamburger comes from cattle, usually beef cattle. The meat is ground (pulverized by cutting it into small pieces by a meat grinder), formed into patties, and then fried or grilled. Beef is in the meat food group and is high in protein, iron, vitamins, and minerals that the body needs each day. Buffalo meat may also be made into ground meat patties.

Cheese. Cheese is made from the curd (solids) of milk. The curd is separated from the watery part of the milk, which is called whey. It is then pressed into a hoop or a mold and left to ripen or age to develop flavor. Although most cheese is made from cows' milk, cheese can also be made from the milk of goats, camels, sheep, buffalo, or reindeer. Cheese provides protein, minerals (calcium, phosphorus), and vitamins (vitamin A and riboflavin). Cheese is in the dairy food group, also called the milk group.

Bacon. Bacon is the meat of a grown pig called a hog. Lower fat or leaner bacon is now available and may be considered a meat group food. Bacon has traditionally been considered a part of the other category or extra food group because the fat and calories in it outweigh the nutritional value.

Tomatoes. A tomato is a fruit that grows on a vine. It is green until it ripens. Then, it turns red or yellow. Tomatoes are a good source of vitamins A and C.

Lettuce. The type of lettuce most often used on a hamburger grows in a head and is called iceberg lettuce. It has crisp leaves and is pale green in color. Other types of lettuce are used in salads and grow in bunches. They have darker green or purplish-green leaves. Lettuce is a vegetable and a good source of vitamins.

Onions. Onions are members of the lily family. Their bulbs grow below the ground. Onions have a strong taste and smell, although some varieties are sweeter than others, and some are milder than others. Onions are vegetables and a good source of vitamins.

Pickles. Pickles are made from cucumbers, which are vegetables. The cucumbers are usually cooked and then packed in vinegar and spices. Some pickles are sweet, and some are sour.

Ketchup. Ketchup is made from tomatoes that are cooked and then mixed with vinegar. Onions, sweet peppers, spices, and sugar are added for flavor.

Mustard. Mustard seeds may be yellow or brown. The seeds are ground into powder and then mixed with vinegar and spices (such as garlic) to make a mustard spread.

Mayonnaise. Mayonnaise is made from eggs that are whipped with oil, spices, and vinegar or lemon juice. The mixture is then used as a salad dressing or as a sandwich spread.

Vinegar. Vinegar, which is made from apple juice, is used to make mustard, ketchup, and mayonnaise. Vinegar adds flavor and helps preserve food.

Note: Because the amount of pickles, onions, ketchup, mustard, and mayonnaise added to a hamburger is small, these foods do not add a significant amount of nutrition to the daily food intake and are in the other or extra food group.

Assessment

Assessment may be done with writing assessments and graphic organizers. The writing assessments vary according to the ability and level of the class. Scoring guides are part of the assessment process.

Students can make group books. Each student chooses (or is assigned) an ingredient of the burger and then writes about it.

Students can research a specific ingredient of the hamburger or research all of the ingredients in their favorite hamburger to find additional information, such as key nutrients or caloric content.

Students can also write about their favorite hamburger meal. They can tell what foods would be included in this meal and the food groups they represent. They can evaluate the meal and specify what they would need to eat and drink with it to have a balanced meal with all the five food groups represented. This activity could be worded as a performance-based student prompt.

Graphic organizers, such as Venn diagrams, can be used to illustrate the source of each part of the burger. Tables or charts could be used to illustrate the part of the plant—fruit, seed, leaf, root, or stem—each ingredient comes from.

Animal Source	Plant and Animal Source	Plant Source
Hamburger Bacon Cheese	Mayonnaise	Bun Tomatoes Mustard Ketchup Lettuce Onions Pickles

Cards with names of foods and food groups (make sure there are enough food group cards to match all the foods) can be used to play a memory game.

Fruit Group	Meat Group	Dairy Group	Vegetable Group	Bread Group	Other
Tomatoes	Hamburger Bacon	Cheese	Lettuce Onions	Bun	Mayonnaise Ketchup Mustard Pickles

Math and writing skills can be included with multitask performance assessments. Students can do the following math and writing activities:

- Students can write about the ingredients they like on their hamburgers.
- Students can survey the class to determine the ingredients students like on their burgers. Graphs can be made to illustrate the results.
- Students can compute the cost of their favorite hamburger with all ingredients, given individual costs.
- Students can research to find the caloric value of individual foods and compute the total calorie count.
- Students can construct tables and bar graphs to illustrate the ingredients students like on their burgers.

Accommodations for Students With Diverse Learning Needs

The teacher will need to read student prompts and explain new vocabulary words to students with delayed reading or vocabulary skills. Picture cards may be used instead of word cards for vocabulary and graphic organizers. Beginning readers can make their own word cards to label the parts of the hamburger. Kinesthetic learners benefit from a hands-on activity of making models.

Food Activity: Hamburger Snacks

Miniature hamburger snacks can be made for a food activity.

Ingredients

1 chocolate mint cookie (Keebler Grasshopper cookies work well) for the hamburger

2 vanilla wafers for the bun

Red icing for ketchup

Yellow icing for mustard

Directions: Place the hamburger between the pieces of bun and then add the extras:

Little squares of green fruit snacks for lettuce (or use green icing)

Little squares of yellow fruit snacks for cheese

White icing for mayonnaise

Brown icing for bacon

Note: Icing in the squeezable tubes works better than spreadable icing.

Agriculture Connections

Art Linkletter may have coined the phrase "kids say the darndest things," but it is just as true today as it was when the phrase became popular. For example, an eight-year-old girl explained that farmers grow grains and crops to make their fields look pretty. A second-grade boy thought milk came from a faucet in the back of a grocery store. "You know," the boy continued, "the faucet next to the water faucet."

I soon realized that many students are naive about agriculture and the importance of agriculture in their lives. To advance agricultural literacy in my primary classroom I created miniunits that emphasize the importance of agriculture, not only in Missouri but also across the United States. These miniunits make agriculture connections: They inform students of the connection agriculture has not only to our food supply but also to our supply of clothing, housing materials, fuel, medicine, and so on. Environmental preservation—the need to reduce, reuse, and recycle—is an important aspect of some of these connections.

The miniunits and lessons I teach are based on the following comprehensive objectives:

1. To increase students' knowledge of where agricultural products come from and the steps necessary in getting them from farm to market to consumer

2. To enhance students' understanding of the contribution of U.S. agriculture to the nation's supply of food, clothing, fuel, housing materials, medicine, and so on

3. To improve students' reading, writing, science, math, social studies, health, and nutrition knowledge by reading and performing activities that reinforce and enrich learning about plants, animals, and nutrition

These miniunits incorporate varied instructional methods—oral discussion, cooperative learning activities, videos, hands-on activities, demonstrations, food and cooking activities, literature, and writing activities. Some also include demonstrations, experiments, performance-based assessments, art activities, math activities (e.g., estimation, measuring, charting, graphing), and other learning strategies. These varied methods address different learning modalities by providing visual, auditory, tactile, and kinesthetic experiences. Thus they can be adapted to all learners and all areas of instruction. For example, in math we practice critical-thinking skills with a problem of the day, for example, "Ms. McDonald had 8 chickens. If each chicken lays 5 eggs a week, how many eggs would she have in 1 week?"

These cross-curricular miniunits consist of short lessons that can be adjusted to fit a teacher's time frame: They may be taught in thirty minutes or in a couple of hours and may be divided into lessons for one or more afternoons. The miniunits are incorporated into curriculum and thematic units I already teach. Corresponding literacy centers, learning centers, bulletin boards and displays, and other enrichment activities enhance and extend the lessons.

I have developed lessons titled "Where Does Your Burger Come From?" "What Comes From a Farm?" "Where Do Your Jeans Come From?" as well as other lessons on pigs, ice cream, milk, chocolate, peanuts, cranberries, corn, popcorn, cotton, wool, pumpkins, apples, honey, wheat, carrots, farm animals, farm equipment and safety, and potatoes.

Critical-thinking and literacy skills are incorporated into these interesting and challenging cross-curricular lessons. Students can also apply these agricultural connections to their everyday life experiences and real-life situations. Thus, they see a purpose to the learning.

The units address district, state, and national education standards. The unit objectives correlate with the local district standards, which align with the Missouri Show Me Standards, and national education standards. For example, the objectives from the "Where Does Your Burger Come From?" unit, which are listed at the beginning of this section, address state and national standards.

The students continue to say the darndest things. Once during a honey unit, when I was displaying beehives on a bee farm, a student remarked, "So that's what those are! Mr. Jones [a neighbor] has some of those." Truly, Mr. Jones (and yes, that's his real name) has bees, hives, and sells honey. Another student connected to the pictures of a pumpkin farm when he realized he had been by one on numerous occasions but didn't know what the "orange things in the field" were. The most amazing responses came when students learned that the husband of one of the school's teachers had had open-heart surgery several years ago, replacing one of his heart valves with a bovine valve.

Students are also intrigued to learn about the uses for the by-products of these agricultural products. For example, they are amazed to find out that cows provide leather. The students learn about different types of corn and how it is used. They learn that corn by-products can be used to make paints, plastics, and gasoline. They dissolve biodegradable packing material and learn that corn by-products make this possible. They learn that corn syrup comes from corn and is used as a sweetener in many products. My students realized at lunch one day that corn syrup was in their chocolate milk, and a few days later they noticed that soda contained corn syrup. (Students are becoming label readers at eight years of age—yeah!)

I am also able to educate the parents by sending home information sheets regarding the unit we are studying. I encourage the students to tell their parents about the lessons and share (even read together) the information sheets I send home. I get interesting feedback from the parents. Many of the parents express that they, too, have learned new things.

The students and I also discuss some economic factors relating to agriculture and their daily lives. We compare the cost of drinks, such as milk and soda, in a math lesson. Through this activity they are able to grasp a simple understanding of supply and demand.

I hope my agriculture connection lessons make them more aware of the many ways that agriculture touches their lives each day.

Enhancing Curriculum Through a Student Space Program

Mona Sue McPherson
Hendersonville, Tennessee

From the first day of school I knew Bart was different. Bart was a quiet, unassuming, responsible student. He was not totally accepted by his peers who jokingly referred to him as a walking encyclopedia. He could seemingly be absorbed in a book during a lecture but would give a detailed, technical answer to any question I asked. Rarely in my years of teaching have I encountered a student like Bart. Having Bart left me grappling with the lack of challenging content for this gifted student. He had an insatiable appetite for science, especially physics. It was difficult to challenge him; he clearly needed additional academic encouragement.

With thirty-five students in my class it was a major challenge to provide learning experiences to students with such a wide range of abilities. Bart made As on all my assignments and 100s on tests. I feared he was bored and felt I must enhance his curriculum. Through a professional organization, the National Science Teachers Association, I learned about an academic competition—the Student Space Involvement Program (SSIP), developed by NASA and the National Science Teachers Association. Students designed scientific projects to send on board the space shuttle for this contest. I thought this contest might help to expand Bart's horizons and encourage his individual research in physics.

I tapped into his inclination to dream of new concepts through the SSIP. My theory was correct, and I saw a spark of enthusiasm and excitement. He chose an appropriate topic, one in which he had an interest—plasma physics. With little encouragement, he entered the contest. He needed help in organizational skills to effectively summarize, organize, and integrate his concepts, but now he had a motivating reason to learn these skills. Bart was a regional winner, awarded with the opportunity to visit a nearby NASA center and present his project to the judges, a panel of NASA scientists and engineers.

The oral presentation was an obstacle for him. This shy young man worked arduously to overcome his fear of speaking and develop communication skills. He gave a wonderful presentation and answered queries from the scientists with confidence. He gained much more than regional SSIP status with this honor. His self-confidence and self-esteem soared. He won the admiration and respect of his peers. His interest in physics led him to enter a career in that field.

▧   Bringing the Outside Into Your Classroom to Reach Students of All Levels

Patrick Boehmer
Carrington, North Dakota

What do you do when you are studying animals and plants in your curriculum and you are in the middle of North Dakota in the winter?

As a science teacher for over twenty years, I was continually faced with this problem. No matter how many videos we watched or how many pictures we saw, it wasn't as effective as viewing the real thing. For students on the lower end of the learning scale, relating to what they couldn't see and touch was an even greater challenge.

Ten years ago I decided to try something different. Instead of just talking about an animal or plant, I decided to bring some life into the classroom. I started small, bringing in a ten-gallon fish tank with some goldfish. It started something different, and kids had questions. Why does that fish do that? What is growing on the sides of the aquarium? Why does the water get cloudy? Will those fish have babies? These questions provided tremendous educational moments. They brought our lecture topics to life and enabled kids to see connections. Having life in the classroom provided opportunities for research, cooperative learning, presentations, group discussions, and real-life applications of student learning. Most important was that the activities involved students at all levels of learning.

Each type of learner found something to hang on to. Each student found a place in the educational process. The approach also changed some of my assessment processes to include more rubrics and graded projects. The feedback from parents has always been very positive as well, as students go home with stories of what happened that day.

Over the years my experiment has blossomed. My next addition was a hamster that promptly had babies. We learned all about reproduction and economics (getting several for the price of one and selling them). We even discussed adoption and how to get rid of fourteen hamsters. After that came the twenty-gallon tropical fish tank, three newts, three anoles, a giant centipede, a tarantula, a crayfish, several different plants, two turtles, a rat, and several temporary visitors. Each of these organisms brought a new set of questions and a new set of learning experiences to the classroom.

This year I reached for a completely different experience. I found that teaching students about ocean creatures when you live near the geographic center of North America presents many challenges, especially given that many of my students have never been to the ocean. This year I decided to bring the ocean to them. I wrote a grant for $2,000 to purchase and establish a seventy-five-gallon saltwater tank with marine vertebrates and invertebrates in my classroom. What a tremendous experience! From the initial setup, to all of the cycling that must occur as the tank becomes ready to accept organisms, to the addition of the organisms, it has been truly amazing. Students come into the classroom early just to see what is happening in the tank that day.

The success of the aquarium has even branched out to the elementary teachers who are now bringing their students over to see the science room and all the living things in it. The most important aspect to me is that even students who seemed disinterested in science are now excited about it. They spend their free time watching the tank life, and the approach allows the class to talk about life processes in a manner that students of all levels can relate to. I even hear students sharing information that they have researched independently.

It is important to note that this method of teaching may not be appropriate for all situations. It takes a great deal of time to care for all the organisms. This is a year-round job. I have found that, for safety reasons, I must be very careful about what I bring into the classroom. Some schools or communities may not allow certain organisms to be brought in. It can also be expensive without some financial assistance. If you choose to try it, remember to start small and understand that it takes a lot of patience.

Bringing life into your classroom can be an incredible tool for teaching students of all levels. It can also be a great method for standards-based and cooperative learning. It provides an opportunity for interdisciplinary studies and projects. So if you are looking for a new way to reach students, try putting a little life in your classroom.

Reaching All Learners: One Approach

Loretta Loykasek
Burleson, Texas

Don McLean's song "American Pie" was rewritten using the forest biome as lyrics. A diary written as if the author were Jane Goodall was turned in describing her daily study of gorillas and chimpanzees in Africa. An elaborate model of the chickenpox virus was constructed to illustrate one student's research. Gregor Mendel's discoveries regarding genes and heredity were detailed in a newspaper replicating one from the 1860s. A cake detailing the structures of a cell was shared with the class. These are just a few of the creative, innovative projects that my students complete each six weeks after researching a given topic in Pre-Advanced Placement (Pre-AP) Biology.

I require my Pre-AP Biology students to research a topic relevant to our studies in biology each six weeks. In an effort to make learning more rigorous and show students how what is learned today will relate to their jobs in the future, I have integrated the core subject areas and the career themes of each academy at our high school into these projects. The projects integrate principles of Gardner's multiple intelligences theory and Taylor's product grid with project themes related to biology—biomes, viral diseases, scientists who have contributed to the field of biology, the cell, immigrant or native plants, and invertebrates. All of these topics are broad enough to give the students vast choices, which appeal to their varied interests and learning styles.

After choosing and researching their chosen topic, students are given a list of products from which they may select the product they will submit for evaluation. Products are based on Gardner's multiple intelligences theory as decribed at a Roger Taylor[1] workshop I attended at the Sixth Annual Academic/Career/Technology Integrated Curriculum Conference hosted by the National School Conference Institute in New Orleans, Louisiana. Taylor's product grid lists ten to thirty product choices for each of the eight intelligences. I teach ninth-grade students, so I have narrowed the list and limited students to certain choices in terms of appropriateness to the topic. This format discourages plagiarism because students must take material they have researched and present it in a creative manner. Creativity and innovative approaches are promoted when students are allowed choice in the topic and their finished product.

Students are given a grading rubric outlining the parameters of their project when I assign it. In this way they are aware of what is expected of them and can ask questions as they research their topic. To conclude the assignment, students are required to complete a self-evaluation of their efforts and their final product before turning in the project. I receive many interesting comments from this self-evaluation, ranging from, "I thought this was going to be boring, but found it to be interesting" to "It's hard to find information on a buttercup flower." Throughout my teaching career I have required students to research various topics in biology; however, using the multiple intelligences technique not only improved the quality of the projects I receive but also sparked student interest by addressing their individual learning styles and capitalizing on their strengths. Students eagerly anticipate their research projects each six weeks and I look forward to creative, diverse products that show commitment and effort.

Note

1. For information, contact Dr. T. Roger Taylor, Curriculum Design for Excellence, Inc., P.O. Box 4505, Oak Brook, IL 60522.

Teaching Chemistry-Challenged Students

Julie Gaubatz
San Antonio, Texas

For many students, especially those experiencing difficulty with math or abstract thinking skills, high school chemistry may seem like an insurmountable challenge. One difficulty with chemistry is students' limited real-life exposure to its basic concepts: Most students bring less everyday familiarity with chemistry with them to class than they do to biology or physics (the latter of which is also more visual than chemistry). In addition, students' parents rarely remember enough of their own high school chemistry to help them study at home. Chemistry is often technical, esoteric, and abstract—even more so when presented in the confines of a classroom. However, I have found that even chemistry-challenged students can learn the fundamentals of chemistry by grappling almost immediately with its relevance to provocative real-world problems. I use a teaching technique that asks students to consider real-life, ecological, and epidemiological/medical problems, for which chemistry is a powerful tool. This strategy empowers students to use their learning right away, foregrounding the relevance of chemical equations and molecular structures and demonstrating that chemistry is important for real-life situations beyond their bathrooms and kitchens. My basic strategy invites students to consider a real-world problem that they must learn and use chemistry concepts to solve. Working in collaborative groups, students develop and present proposals for solving the problem as if they were a panel of experts called in for help. The proposals are assessed not only for their integration of chemistry concepts but also for their social and political feasibility, their clarity of design, and their presentational coherence.

Stoichiometry, for example, is one of the most difficult topics we cover in our high school chemistry course. After learning its basics students typically apply stoichiometry concepts to various labs. While this strategy allows students to gain hands-on experience with the topic, most fail to see how it possibly could be important to anyone's life outside of the classroom. At this point it is easy to lose students who are struggling, who may not see the importance of stoichiometry, or who feel there is no room for them in the field of chemistry. Before they reach this point, I present students with pictures of one of our state's most visually dramatic parks, Big Bend National Park in south-west Texas. We look at stunning pictures of Big Bend's vistas and wildlife and discuss its uniqueness as one of the few unspoiled areas of our state.

I then tell students about a fast-emerging threat to Big Bend's beauty: thick clouds of pollution drifting from factories south of the border, which, on many days, completely occlude its views. I pose a question to my students: What can we do about this? After brainstorming with their groups, students quickly realize that we can't simply tell another country (partly for economic reasons) to shut down their polluting factories.

I then give the students their assignment: The State of Texas has hired you and your team to help solve this problem. Your team must come up with a politically and scientifically feasible plan and present your proposals in the next class session. I give the students a brief of essential information, including chemical equations, which may or may not be helpful in their efforts, along with the cost of various chemicals and equipment.

As they review the given materials and explore the topic with their groups, it becomes clear that by using a chemical reaction at the factory, the pollutant can be drastically reduced. Students then realize that to make their findings feasible, they must use stoichiometry, along with a budget, if the factories are going to accept their proposal. The lesson ends with student groups presenting their proposals to the class as if they were a panel of experts competing for the factory's and the government's approval.

A second unit that follows the same pattern is based on the tragedy that occurred in 1986 in West Africa's Lake Nyos valley. To introduce the lesson, students are given a brief overview of the observations made by visitors to Lake Nyos on the morning after the tragedy, where they found whole populations of villagers dead, along with their livestock and wild animals. No noticeable smell was in the air, no disease was apparent, and no violence seemed to have occurred. It looked as if everything had dropped dead without warning or panic. However, to many observers, Lake Nyos itself seemed different. Near the lake a strong sulfurous smell was evident, and the lake had changed from beautifully clear to muddy and clouded. As students attempt to answer their questions about what could have caused the Lake Nyos tragedy, they are given "confidential governmental briefings" based on actual eyewitness testimony and hypothetical yet realistic empirical data from which they must generate their hypotheses. Once students have had sufficient time to digest their briefing materials and discuss the initial hypotheses, they are encouraged to explore various laboratory stations and complete background research activities in a student-directed, teacher-facilitated fashion. Students move from one station to the next at their own pace, in any order with which they feel comfortable.

At the guided laboratory stations, students observe various chemical phenomena, including gases rising out of liquids when pressure is decreased, carbon dioxide's acidic properties, and that, although gases are less dense than water, some are lighter (less dense) than air, while some are heavier (more dense) than air. They also explore the basic geological properties of the lake area along with the cultural and political aspects of northwestern Cameroon, where Lake Nyos is located. All of these learning/lab station activities are brief, and students change activities often, which keeps their interest high.

Students use the information gained from their laboratory explorations and background research to construct a hypothesis that might explain the Lake Nyos tragedy and devise a culturally and politically sensitive method to prevent future similar tragedies from occurring in Africa. Together, these activity-based lessons stimulate students' interest in chemistry by illustrating why its methods are essential for solving real-life problems. The Lake Nyos incident intrigues nearly everyone who has heard about it: A mysterious tragedy materialized suddenly and left just as suddenly, leaving virtually no trace of its origins. The presentation of this data in the form of a "confidential governmental briefing" captures students' interest and motivates them to use their learning opportunities in classroom lab stations to solve the Lake Nyos mystery. My requirement that students develop culturally and politically sensitive solutions to these problems also brings the parameters of real-world science into the classroom: Scientists perform their work not in abstract isolation but in living, dynamic human societies in which their findings and ideas ultimately are accepted or denied. This recognition also allows students to think about their own cultural backgrounds and to seriously consider the cultural backgrounds of other people in the world.

In addition, I have found that cumulating these lessons with creative presentations gives students the opportunity to showcase their creative sides, either through their visual or oral presentations. It's a time for them to have fun with what they've learned on that day (the final day of the lesson, they are the experts). It's their opportunity to acknowledge and celebrate their successes, sometimes only partial, in solving the problems they encounter.

These lessons, along with others, help take the dryness and the intimidation out of high school chemistry. Students begin to view chemistry as a valuable tool for interesting, important situations, not simply as a self-contained academic discipline. While some students are able to see the beauty of chemistry and the mathematics that allow them to learn about the universe, other students require personal involvement and a touch of reality that make science both achievable and welcoming.

Helpful Tips

Chemistry courses, like many other science courses, can be perceived by some students as elitist. Some students think that only the best and brightest can enjoy chemistry, but all students should have the opportunity to see the wonders of the world that chemistry reveals and be invited to participate in scientific inquiry. It is possible to maintain high academic standards while still including and welcoming all students to the pleasures of scientific discovery. Using activities that deviate from the normal lecture/lab setup of science courses, I try to give all of my students the chance to participate in class and express their talents. When developing my lessons, I try to hit students' diverse learning and personality styles, developing activities that I may not have found enjoyable as a student (I preferred the lecture/lab sequence) but that I know will be inviting to others. This process stretches my creativity to think outside the lecture/lab box, and it forces me to recalibrate the calendar to cover critical topics. Despite all the work, I am consistently rewarded when I give all students the opportunity to be successful and to express their diverse talents in my science classes.

Using Culminating Activities to Reach All Learners

Lorine M. Lee
Flowery Branch, Georgia

Throughout my years of teaching I have had the opportunity to instruct students from a variety of backgrounds and abilities. My first year of teaching was a difficult one. I taught five classes per day, three of them regular education classes and two project success classes. In these two types of classes were a variety of issues I had to deal with. Some of the issues I dealt with each day involved family problems, student drug abuse, hyperactivity, and low achievement. After trying the traditional method of teaching—read the book, answer the questions, teach the material—I realized this method was not effective for my students. So I began to explore my options. During my exploration, I began to work with another teacher on an activity that involved different learning styles. This activity, called a culminating activity, seemed to be the right solution for the learning issues I observed in my classroom. The first time I used this activity I was amazed. While all of the students did not perform to their greatest capacity, they did improve. Improvement was the key. As I observed the changes in my students I also felt their success. I became a facilitator and coach in the classroom.

So the question is, what is a culminating activity? A culminating activity is a planned exploration of a product in which the final step involves an exciting final action. In other words, our activities throughout the week, two weeks, or the month focus on a particular goal or end product and the resulting activity. What do I mean by that? Read further as I outline the process.

First I ask myself, "What do the students need to achieve?" (i.e., "What does the state require?"). Then I ask myself how I can get my students to understand these concepts while addressing all their learning styles. Then I go to work designing culminating activities. The first culminating activity I designed involved rockets and Newton's laws of motion. I first developed a guide that would lead my students through the process. The guide involved different activity steps, the first being to research rockets and their design. The next activity involved reviewing the facts of Newton's laws of motion and the discovery of how the laws apply to rockets (this is also done through research). Through exploration and a minimal amount of lecture my students write a paper describing what they've learned (linguistic/auditory). Once their papers have been read and approved, students move on to the next step—a laboratory activity.

The laboratory activity contains integrated mathematical analysis, requiring students to find the height of objects around the school using the Pythagorean theorem. Once done the students can use the knowledge they gained to assess the performance of their rockets on launching day. Further, students use mathematical equations to calculate the speed of their rocket (spatial, logical).

To learn the scientific aspects of speed my students also participate in labs that involve speed calculators. We have running races (kinesthetic).

The students race each other and determine their speeds by mathematically analyzing their distance and time. To reduce learner anxiety, students for this activity are volunteers from the classroom.

Brainstorming is the next step in the culminating activity process. As the students move through this step, different learning styles emerge. Students must assimilate the information they have learned through research and investigation to design a rocket. They must first brainstorm ideas about their rocket design and draw eight different sketches. These sketches, called thumbnail sketches, are used for idea generation. Once the sketches are drawn and approved, the students use them to decide which model would be the best to build.

Once their decision is made, they draw a rough sketch of their rocket. The final drawing, called a working drawing, is used as a guide for rocket building. This drawing has all of the dimensions and the materials that they will use in the construction process (aesthetic/visual). After approval of the working drawing the students move to the next step—building their product. The students' guide contains information regarding material and size restrictions, which must be followed. The students bring building materials to class and spend classroom time constructing their rockets (aesthetic/visual). Once their rockets are built, it's time for takeoff. We spend a day doing our culminating activity—launching rockets and assessing performances.

All students learn differently. This type of activity accommodates all learning styles, from linguistic to kinesthetic. Culminating activities can also be adjusted to enhance different levels of understanding. These activities can be modified to accommodate the needs of the most gifted student and the most challenged. I use this activity and others similar to it with students in project success classes (challenged learners) and with students in my physics class, both of which experience a sense of accomplishment and a feeling of self-worth. Each student can find his or her niche using these activities.

When grading, teachers can adjust the focus of the grade accordingly. For example, when I team teach these activities with the drafting teacher, I focus on grading the science students for their science understanding, while the drafting teacher focuses the grading on drawing and building activities. Further, if a student is more linguistically inclined, teachers can adjust grading in a manner that enhances this ability.

One of the major concerns using this type of activity is student follow-through and time. The teacher should be realistic regarding the time needed for all learners to achieve the goal. Some students may be done in a week, while others may take longer; however, if teachers are good facilitators, they can adjust the schedule accordingly. I have found that when I am facilitating these activities I spend time guiding the students who need help, while the others have the freedom to work according to their abilities. If the deadline needs to be extended, I extend it; if the students finish faster than expected, I adjust the schedule. Keeping in time with all of the students is essential.

Now, seven years later, I am still achieving success in my classroom by using culminating activities. I use them with as many science topics as I can and develop more when I feel there is a need. Students who participate in these activities achieve success through self-guided, teacher-coached activities designed to enhance their individual learning style.

The Middle School Means Success Program

P. J. Godwin
Birmingham, Alabama

I have been teaching science and chemistry at the Alabama School of Fine Arts (ASFA) in Birmingham for the last five years. All of my students are majoring in one of the five fine arts offered—creative writing, dance, music, theatre arts, or visual arts. Consequently, one of the last things on their minds is science class or chemistry problems. My teaching style has had to adapt over the years to reach these artistic, creative kids with such an analytical, left-brained subject.

Early on I noticed that a few of my kids would come in with an attitude that they couldn't do it. Their art was so drilled into them for so long that the idea of stepping out of their comfort zone was somewhat frightening. Combine this attitude with the intimidation felt by new seventh graders, who are in school with juniors and seniors, and the atmosphere can be very daunting.

One of the first goals I have every year is to make sure the middle school students do not feel alienated or intimidated. I realize I am just one teacher, so I developed the MSMS program—Middle School Means Success program. It gave not only the students but also the parents a sense of belonging in the ASFA community and gave them a sense of being special. A newsletter was created, focusing specifically on what the middle school students were doing. E-mail communication between parents and teachers became frequent and a great way to head off potential problems before they started. Overall the program gave the younger kids a sense of belonging.

Another constant goal of mine is to be sure my students do not leave their artistic talents at the door. Any chance I get I try to work creative projects and ideas into their science class. In chemistry we finished making pigments and paints through a variety of chemical reactions. This project was received well by all children, not only the kids majoring in visual arts. Every now and then I assign my older chemistry students a project in which they have to artistically represent a chemical element. They are not limited to their major for this project. Dancers may draw; actors may compose. But they have to do a little research first to find out facts about the element. This gives them a chance to see the constant connection between art and science, an idea that is part of ASFA's mission statement. Plus, it gives me some cool art to hang on my walls! When I'm asked, "What's that?" I can reply, "Plutonium!"

In the younger grades I try and work in creative projects as much as possible. Even giving them a chance to color a graph they made of the ocean floor is art to them. Bonus opportunities are given in my class if they compose and perform a song in *Schoolhouse Rock* fashion about current material we are studying. Every quarter there is a major creative project that may focus on one of the fine arts, but it is not repeated over the year. An art project is one; a book of poems or a children's book is another. Most of my students love working with the right side of their brain; they are not too concerned about which field they work in. I have gotten spectacular artwork from writing students and wonderful compositions from actors. They love the chance to show off all their talents, yet they know I never grade them on the talent itself but on the effort they put into it. And they learn the science. Students understand genetics after the superhero project, where they have to pick superhero parents and mate them. They remember the nutrient project, where they created journals. They succeed on final exams and standardized tests because they have something visual to think back on. My constant challenge to myself is to teach the way they learn if they can't learn the way I teach.

Helpful Tips

Anything can be a creative project. We were discussing the ocean floor when I decided to take a class period and have them design an underwater city. But the project had to be viable, considering what they already learned about ocean water and its inhabitants. When studying energy sources, my students have to take something that runs on electricity or batteries and modify its design so that it runs on some other source. We write cinquains of science, which are ordered, five-line poems that reemphasize what they have learned about a topic. Skits are performed; truly awful songs are composed to remember facts. Be silly, be unusual, be a goof, be "not well," grab their attention by any means necessary and never let go.

An Out of This World Experience!

Jennifer Linrud
Wichita, Kansas

"Begin countdown to liftoff—10 . . . 9 . . . 8 . . . 7 . . . 6 . . . 5 . . . We have main engine start . . . 2 . . . 1 . . . 0 . . . SRB ignition—We have liftoff!"

Amidst the cheering throughout Mission Control, the space shuttle completes its roll maneuver and thus begins its fantastic voyage into low-Earth orbit. There, astronauts will complete their mission of repairing a damaged solar panel on the International Space Station and conducting biomedical experiments to determine the effects of weightlessness on the human body.

To the casual observer, this scenario may sound like a routine launch and flight plan at NASA. However, this launch did not take place at Kennedy Space Center, and, while the mission was a resounding success, it did not actually occur in space. Instead, all events occurred in a classroom on the campus of Wichita Collegiate Middle School in Wichita, Kansas.

The Idea

As a middle school team member, I have worked with other academic teachers to design interdisciplinary units, several of which involved a simulated experience for our students. Simulations allow students to take ownership in their learning, giving them responsibility for their specific role within the group and allowing them to become participants rather than passive listeners or observers. Specific roles can be tailored to each individual learner so that all students can be successful. For example, in a simulation involving the Underground Railroad, talented art students sketch maps, while students interested in math take azimuth and bearing readings to show student "slaves" where to go. These units were so popular with the kids that I decided to involve my science students in a space shuttle simulation.

Throughout my six years as a science teacher, I've observed that space is a natural motivator for middle schoolers—something about the mystery and inherent danger of space flight is alluring to most kids. However, it can be difficult to get students past the bad science to which they are constantly exposed—our society is so inundated with movies and video games portraying false scientific ideas that children often have a skewed perception of the challenges and realities of our current space program. Many of my students this year were surprised to learn that the shuttle cannot go to other planets or travel at light speed.

Because of these misperceptions, I began the six-week space shuttle unit by teaching the basics about the shuttle itself. We learned about the shuttle's design, its uses and benefits, and the effect of microgravity on materials and people. Some of the activities we completed included building Alka-Seltzer rockets, making scale model shuttles, creating edible satellites, designing robotic arms with end effectors, researching past missions by reading NASA press kits on the Internet, and conducting spatial orientation labs. Therefore, when it came time to introduce the simulation, students already had solid background knowledge with which to make informed decisions. This was very important, since my role at that time shifted from teacher to facilitator. Students now had to solve problems on their own, using current research or the knowledge they obtained from earlier activities.

Building the Simulator

To build an enclosed structure to serve as our space shuttle, I enlisted the aid of a local automotive repair shop owner. Together we designed a shuttle with two decks, a payload bay, and sleeping compartments for twenty-four-hour simulations. Parents and local businesses got together and funded the project. Our Mission Control was located in an adjacent classroom, and I obtained headset two-way radios so that the Mission Control crew could communicate with the crew inside the shuttle.

However, even though our simulations were done using an expensive simulator, teachers can conduct inexpensive simulations by putting together cardboard boxes, PVC pipe, or inflated trash bags to make an enclosed structure. The value in doing simulations in the classroom is not in having the most current technology or an expensive simulator; rather, it is in giving students ownership in their respective responsibilities and giving some insight into real-world career options.

The Curriculum

In designing the curriculum for the simulation, I tried to make everything as realistic as possible. Each mission included elements of actual shuttle missions, including launch, landing, experiments, medical assessments, and so on. I also wanted each child to take ownership in the mission, so I assigned different positions and assignments to each student. Some of the positions included astronaut (commander, pilot, mission specialist, payload specialist, CAPCOM), flight director, flight dynamics officer, engineer, public affairs officer, correspondent, flight surgeon, graphic design artist, and several others.

Students interested in becoming astronauts had to apply for their positions. The application process included requirements similar to those of NASA: Applicants had to write an essay, obtain recommendations, pass physical tests, and maintain a high grade point average. In addition, they had to design an experiment to conduct in space. This process allowed students to gain real-world experience in preparing an application, asking for recommendation letters from adults, and conducting research into essay questions and lab reports. Although no academic credit was given for the extra work required to submit an astronaut application, nearly half of my students applied for the few astronaut slots available. Applications were independently judged by adult volunteers in the community to ensure the absence of any bias on my part or that of the teaching staff. For other positions, students listed their top three choices, and I made every effort to assign them a job within those choices.

Throughout our classroom preparation for the simulation, student teams were required to work independently on their assignments. Since each team was working on something different, I couldn't possibly conduct a structured class each day. At first, I was a little uncertain about giving the kids free reign to work—I was sure the period would dissolve into chaos. However, I was surprised to observe how seriously the students took their positions and how well they understood that everyone was important to the success of the mission. An intense spirit of teamwork enveloped my room each day, and the energy was amazing. Many students spent their own time after school and during recess working on their assignments, and several astronaut crews requested time at school on the weekends to gain extra practice with their scripts and experiments.

An Interdisciplinary Experience

While this activity obviously involved scientific concepts, I wanted students to realize that science is really the application of many different disciplines. In other words, they needed a variety of skills to work in the space program. Although each student had different assignments to complete, I attempted to incorporate various disciplines into each one. All students spent time in the computer lab, whether it was creating a PowerPoint presentation, designing a Web page, conducting Internet research, writing lab reports, or downloading pictures of Earth from space to use in Earth observation experiments. Many positions also required the use of problem solving and mathematics. Math was used in determining averages for experiments, for timing abort options during launch, and for constructing glove boxes.

Writing was incorporated in every position as well. Every two to three days each team reported to the entire group by writing a Mission Status Report. These reports detailed what had been accomplished, what was yet to be accomplished, and any questions they had for myself or other teams. Reports were then shared and collected at the beginning of the period for grading. The astronauts and flight director were required to keep journals of their experiences, while other positions wrote articles for the school newsletter, prepared presentations for younger children, conducted interviews, and summarized lab experiments. Furthermore, my students responded to more than 200 space questions from first through fourth graders via e-mail.

Students who had previously disliked writing now had a purpose for written expression. Since groups depended on each other for data, written procedures, and summaries of experiments, students understood the importance of quality writing. Those who excelled in written expression helped out those who didn't, pointing out ways to make their writing more clear or expansive.

On the day of the simulation my fifth graders were both nervous and excited. We had equipped Mission Control with a live video feed from the simulator, so parents and other community members could see exactly what was happening inside the shuttle at all times. The *Wichita Eagle* and *Belle Plaine* newspapers covered the event, and several TV stations were on hand to interview astronauts and mission controllers for the nightly news. One station even conducted a live broadcast of the simulation on its noon show.

Conducting a space shuttle simulation is a fantastic way to involve all learners. There is a job for every student. Graphic design artists design mission patches and posters, engineers design and construct space station modules, scientists create experiments, astronauts conduct public relations presentations for elementary students, correspondents create a Web page, life support specialists design and construct spacesuits, and the flight director displays responsible leadership. Everyone is responsible for something important to the mission, and the students quickly learn that they can't be successful without the talent and participation of everyone in the class.

The students took their roles very seriously, many of them actually becoming a member of the space program. As the students for one mission entered the Mission Control room, the flight director stopped all of them at the door for one final word. "You are no longer fifth graders at Collegiate," he told them. "You are now NASA employees. Let's have a successful mission."

The mission was, indeed, a success, and many students now rate the simulation as the best experience of fifth grade. Several students have set their sights on Mars, determined to be the first Americans to set foot on the Red Planet. I've already requested tickets to the launch.

National Standards

This activity incorporates many elements of the National Science Standards. It highlights a portion of all the Teaching Standards; Assessment Standard B; portions of 5–8 Content Standards A, B, and D–G; and Program Standards B and C.

Helpful Tips

Conducting Simulations in the Classroom

1. Learn to step back. For teachers used to controlling the direction of their classes, conducting simulations is especially difficult. It was a real paradigm shift for me to allow students to effectively direct the class, rather than conducting a structured class period each day. It truly is amazing what students can accomplish with minimal structure, as long as they have a clear picture of the expectations involved.

2. Create positions or jobs based on the talents and skill levels of your students. Last year, I created the graphic design artist position specifically for a very talented art student who sometimes had difficulty working closely with others. By working independently on assignments such as the mission patch, he was able to showcase his talent and receive positive recognition from the group as a whole.

(Continued)

3. Create an atmosphere of interdependence. Be sure that students understand the importance of teamwork. Foster their interdependence by making sure that each position depends on at least one other in some capacity. For example, the correspondents must understand the experiments designed by the science team before they can describe them on the Web page. Astronauts must work with the engineers to learn to assemble the space station module on a spacewalk. The meteorologist must discuss the abort landing sites with the flight dynamics officer before he or she can find out the weather conditions at those sites. The list goes on. This gives students a feeling of ownership, as well as a little bit of positive group pressure. I've seen students who never turned in an assignment on time suddenly stay after school to work on something another group needs the next day.

4. Have fun! While simulations require an extraordinary amount of work, they are also very rewarding. It is truly a thrill to see students come alive with excitement over a school activity. Each year, I am reminded that projects like this are the reason I teach.

 **Addressing Gender Equity Issues
Through Alternative Lesson Design Methods**

David Brock
Baltimore, Maryland

My purpose in teaching biology at an all-girl school is to nurture young women to pursue whatever intellectual passions they discover within themselves and to nourish the innate adolescent curiosity that might lead that devotion someday to embrace science. Anyone familiar with a recent U.S. Commission on Civil Rights report knows that a critical challenge facing our society is the continuing low numbers of women entering science research fields; if we are to change this, we must find ways to teach that empower young women to overcome stereotypical barriers and the future hurdles they will face.

In my own career, I have found one such way to accomplish this goal—my approach to lesson design. Instead of presenting material in a manner seen all too often in classrooms, as a kind of dogmatic catechism, with dry textbook readings introducing a flood of abstract ideas and cookbook activities simply confirming the finality of it all, I teach any topic using the methodology of the subject my students are studying. Therefore, since real science is a process, a systematic method for asking and answering questions about the world, I have my students "do" science rather than read about it. The girls in my classroom conjecture and design testable solutions, perform precision measurements and observations, and discover the distinction between raw data and the conclusions drawn from data. I take the stance when developing all my lessons that I should be equipping the children in my classroom to think scientifically rather than just to know scientific things—to understand how to acquire knowledge rather than merely to receive it.

My goal, then, when designing lessons is to do so in such a way that my students write their own textbook rather than read someone else's. By transforming any topic I want mastered into a research question, I enable the young women I teach to explore an idea as if it were new and unknown and, thereby, to make the understanding of it their own. So, for example, if I want children to learn about the fundamental role of DNA in life, I have my class insert extraneous DNA into bacteria and see what happens. Or, if I want them to discover how cells compensate for changes in their external environment, I have the girls place a plant leaf in different solutions under a microscope and describe what happens. By the end of the year I have merely to tell them we are going to study the environmental roles of soil microbes and they are off and experimenting.

Granted, such an approach to lesson design does require the patience to let students work through a problem at their pace rather than the teacher's, and it demands a willingness to allow them to own the responsibility for their own education. Moreover, it challenges me as a teacher to know my subject matter well enough to transform topic ideas into investigative questions. But I have found the rewards for doing so to be immense: Students think—independently, creatively, and analytically. I have found that young women who learn this way learn to love science because for them it is not the work of "some dead White guy" but is instead the work of themselves and their peers. Science comes alive for my girls because they have experienced first-hand what it means to work, to think, and to comprehend in a scientific fashion. I firmly believe that life is not a textbook; it is an adventure, and when science—or anything else—is taught that way, all children become empowered to engage their world in all the imaginative, rational ways the mind allows. They become equipped to transform their lives, their communities, and their society accordingly. And, in the end, isn't that what real teaching is supposed to be—the drawing out in another the capacity as a person to grow and live in a meaningful way?

Helpful Tips

Educators have an awesome power and responsibility, and even after nearly fifteen years of teaching at both the university and precollege levels, in public, private, rural, and inner city schools, I still remain humbled at this potential we have as teachers to affect others. What is more, I remain anxious after all these years that I can be worthy of the trust implicit in such power, and, because the anxiety of that trust remains a very real part of who I am, I would like to offer a story out of my own teaching career, which contains, I believe, the wisest, most important advice I have ever received about this profession.

As an undergraduate, I once overheard the renowned art historian Norris K. Smith make a comment to a group of medical students that the purpose in life is not so much to be a well human being but to learn to be human well. I did not give the thought much attention at the time, but many years later, shortly after winning my first national teaching award, I heard something that taught me the wisdom of what Smith once said. I had returned to my own high school after more than a decade to share the news of my award with my tenth-grade English teacher, Karl

---

(Continued)

Krauskopf, and to share with him his own influence on me as a teacher. It remains a special moment in my life and a special memory, but it was not until I was getting back into my car at the end of our visit that the real power of both teaching and Smith's comment hit me. Mr. Krauskopf's parting words to me were "Always remember, David, care at least a little more about the kids than you do about the subject." I knew then, as he reached out to mold me yet again, that what all my teachers had really done was to show me how to be human well. May all of our students be able to say the same of each of us someday.

Using Hands-On Science and Math to Engage All Learners

Coleen M. Martin
Chillicothe, Illinois

Students will love science and math and will understand concepts better by using hands-on activities. I have had great success engaging students of all ability levels by using this approach.

Our fifth-grade science curriculum now contains many activities to excite all students. Each fifth grader builds and launches a rocket. These paper rockets are easily and inexpensively made. Students try various combinations of materials on their paper rockets: various tube lengths, different numbers of fins, and different shapes of fins. They also test for center of pressure and center of gravity. As they launch with air pressure, they observe and keep accurate records. After learning the physics of launching rockets, they build a model rocket from a kit. The rocket is constructed according to the directions and then painted. After the students put on the finishing touches, the rockets are ready to be launched. Students learn how the rocket engine is constructed and how it works. Rocket Launch Day is a big event for our school. Parents, grandparents, students, school board members, and sometimes the media join us for the big day.

After completing the rocket unit, we then continue studying physics with the Society of Automotive Engineers' World in Motion program. Students learn about engineering from a volunteer engineer. The miniengineers work in teams to design, build, and test various options on a car made of easily obtained materials. After testing various configurations by adding weight, streamlining, and reducing friction, the students add balloon power. Various nozzles are tested, and the cars compete in the final race for the volunteer engineer. Following the race, the engineer discusses the various choices made by the teams and relates their choices to their car's performance.

When the students build their rockets, they use rulers to measure to fractions of inches. When they test the cars, the teams measure the distance in centimeters. After testing the car three times, the distances are averaged. Thus students find a practical application for the math skills being taught in class.

Many math concepts can be taught using different manipulatives. Pattern blocks are great for teaching fractions and geometric shapes and attributes. The students can discover many fractional relationships among the various pattern blocks. Using the blocks to trace, the children can show proper, improper, and mixed fractions and explain in words the relationships. The pattern blocks are great for discussing the geometric shapes and their attributes.

Color tiles are great for probability activities and fraction problems. Teachers place a variety of color tiles in a paper bag. The students pull one out and identify it. The class keeps track of the number of times each color has been pulled out. After sufficient data has been collected, the students ask algebraic questions: Are there more red blocks than blue? Is blue plus red greater than green? What is the formula, using variables? Students can get very creative in their questioning. After enough algebraic formulas have been identified to solve the problem, tell the students how many tiles are in the bag. Let the teams figure out the number of tiles of each different color. After the problem is solved, explain the probability of pulling out each color and relate the mathematical probability to the experimental probability.

Another great fraction activity also involves using color tiles. The students fill in a rectangle using color tiles. The rectangle must be one-third blue, one-eighth green, and one-sixth red. The rest is yellow.

Students find a common denominator and make equivalent fractions to determine the number of each color tile. Adding the fractions to determine the leftover color is another math skill the students use. Coloring in the rectangle on graph paper requires students to determine the correct dimensions for the rectangle. After doing several problems similar to this one, students can then explain their problem-solving process in writing.

Students love working with different hands-on materials. By making meaningful activities for them to solve, math and science can become much more enjoyable and understandable.

Helpful Tips

- It's always a good idea to try the activity before teaching it.
- Always keep safety in mind when using materials.

▨ Using Checkpoints to Increase Compliance

Brandy Fenenga
Watertown, South Dakota

Frustrated. I couldn't seem to find any other word to describe how I was feeling after grading another group of labs for my learning center science class. This class consisted of twenty-four students, mostly ninth graders, all of them on an Individualized Education Plan (IEP). Grading the labs wasn't the only reason I was frustrated; I had been on edge since teaching a particular class earlier in the day. I had retyped the directions for the class's lab, which were from a middle school science textbook, to try and improve the situation, an attempt that proved unsuccessful. While it is true that you can expect a few questions regarding the procedure, this class's response was ridiculous. Had they read the directions at all or just started mixing stuff together? The goal of the lab was to build a model showing the different layers of the earth using food products. The directions seemed simple enough to me: "Mix the peanut butter and the powdered milk together until it forms a doughlike consistency." So why did I have groups with jelly in their peanut butter or their chocolate chips? Of course, these were all mixed together in a cup and somehow the ball of peanut butter that was to represent the layers of the earth was nowhere to be found. It was as if they had just started putting stuff haphazardly into the paper cup.

So here I was with a whole ninety-minute period wasted, not to mention the $30 that I spent at the grocery store that morning on supplies. I thought that this would be such a great lab and that they would enjoy it. Not one group answered their questions with anything remotely close to what I wanted or with answers that had anything to do with the structure of the earth, which was the whole point of doing the lab.

Where had I gone wrong? I didn't think I could make the directions any simpler. Why couldn't they just read the directions? I was at the point of giving up labs completely. As tempting as this was, I had two big problems with giving up on labs. As a science teacher, I knew it was no way to teach a science class. I also couldn't come up with enough worksheets and seatwork for a ninety-minute class that met daily. This wasn't the first time I had been frustrated with this class. What also bothered me was that I was starting to believe that this was my fault— I was failing as a teacher. I knew I couldn't give labs up, no matter how much I wanted to.

Not only was I having a hard time getting students to read and follow directions, but I was also having difficulty getting them to answer questions about the lab. A few of them simply didn't understand why I wouldn't let them do the lab without any questions at all. The responses I got in the students' summaries often contained only one word, usually "yes" or "no," with little or no thought given to what the question was actually asking. A good example was a lab we had just finished using a hardboiled egg as a model of the earth. I asked, "What does the shell of the egg represent in your model of the earth?" The most common response was not the crust of the earth but "yes" or "the outside of the egg." That I couldn't accept these types of answers didn't seem to matter to the students. In the past when I tried to make them redo their work, most students took the low score instead of spending time redoing the work properly. Not understanding was a poor but common excuse I got when I asked why a question hadn't been completed properly. I never accepted this excuse because this class also has an aide, who is a certified teacher, to help them with their work.

After much thought, I decided to change the way I wrote the procedure for the lab. I had been working hard to break each step down into short, numbered steps. Students had a habit of going from Step 1 to Step 6 without completing the steps in between, so the numbers were replaced with large checkboxes. Before going on to the next step, the checkboxes had to be initialed by either the aide or myself. This seemed to slow students down enough that they weren't rushing through just to get the lab done and turned in. It also gave us a chance to make sure the lab was being done correctly before it was finished and the materials put away. I also started to put the questions in throughout the procedure, so the students' answers could be checked while they did the lab.

I worried that there would be too much off-task behavior while the students waited to have their labs checked. However, the process went better than I thought. The students spent more time answering the questions because they read them while waiting. In some ways, I think the amount of goofing around decreased, even though students actually had to wait longer.

As the year progressed, the reading and following of directions got better, and I still use this format for labs. I gradually increased the number of steps between checkpoints. I still try to place data and questions between checkpoints to make sure that the students understand the reason for doing labs. Getting longer answers still remains a challenge, and we continue to work on that. There are still days when labs go horribly amiss, but this seems to happen less often than it used to.

Helpful Hints

■ Use an outline format, but instead of numbers use checkboxes large enough for teacher initials.

■ Insert as many questions as possible into the procedure. It is easier to check for student understanding while checking to make sure the directions are being followed.

(Continued)

> - Start with very simple directions. I find I often have to rewrite directions that are written at a sixth-grade reading level. As students master the directions at a lower reading level, gradually increase the number of steps between checkpoints.
>
> - Impose consequences for continuing the activity without getting the teacher's initials. In my classroom, going on without teacher approval is the same as goofing around: Students who fail to get approval have to sit at their desks and not complete the lab, which results in a score of zero. If it continues to be a problem, the students can be sent out of the classroom, but I haven't had to resort to this consequence yet.

Making Science Come Alive

Jim Miller
Cle Elum, Washington

Several years ago, another science teacher (the only other science teacher in our high school) and I sat down and decided to tackle a problem: the same students repeatedly failing a required general science course. We also wanted to address the declining enrollment in science. With very little discussion we realized we were trying to teach science the same way—by having students read the book, listen to lectures, answer the questions, and take the test—even though that way did not work for these students the first time. We had the perfect formula to guarantee failure for our struggling students.

I decided I needed to try something different. The first thing to go was the book. I decided that students would journal each day. They would have to write sentences about their learning. I spent several weeks teaching them how to write: not simply writing about what they did but describing what they actually learned and understood. For example, students continually wanted to write, "We learned about acceleration today." After instruction in how to write, students showed more understanding in their journals. For example, students might write, "Now I get it. Acceleration is how much the change in the speed is divided by how long it takes to make that change." This was not easy and still isn't for the students, but they are thoughtful and reflective about what is happening in the class. They search for the main ideas being explored.

Of course, then I had to provide more than facts to the students. By raising the bar for the students, I raised the bar for myself. I had to reflect on the purpose of my lesson and evaluate the importance of each concept. I realized that most of their science consisted of facts, with little emphasis on building an intuitive sense about their world. I made the decision to bar no holds and use every piece of interesting science equipment we had, and I left out all of the mathematical explanations. I realized that using math equations and formulas to explain science concepts for this age group worked for few students. For the rest, trying to learn science concepts using math was like learning the Russian language in a classroom of Japanese-speaking people when your native tongue is English.

We now climb ropes in the gym to study forces and friction, and we roll balls down lunch tables trying to duplicate Galileo's gravity experiments. We make holograms in the classroom. We make motors out of magnet wire, wooden dowels, and paper clips. We design gliders, make buzzers, and make parabolic reflectors. Using kitchen chemicals we explore chemistry and the periodic table. Wiring framed walls (e.g., wiring in a new house) allows us to develop electrical concepts. We become engineers as we take apart and often repair old clocks and lamps. The science around the students comes alive. I've had parents call and tell me that their son or daughter just repaired a light fixture or an electrical switch.

As you might imagine, the students who failed before are now successful. They know and see the purpose in what they are doing. It makes sense for me to teach science in this way to all students. After our science department began teaching with this philosophy, course enrollment surged. Students didn't want to miss out on the fun. For many students, the general science class became their favorite course. Several chose careers related to the course, such as a wiring technician. Special needs students also fared well in this environment. Few other accommodations were necessary as the change in philosophy met their special needs.

CHAPTER 6

Teaching With Styles

 Active Introduction to a New Classroom

Victoria L. Richey
Midwest City, Oklahoma

As each new school year begins, I want the first reactions to my classroom to be excitement, curiosity, and intrigue. Knowing some of my new students by reputation only and not knowing the others at all, I like to set up an atmosphere that will guide me in establishing a learning environment where all students can and will achieve to the best of their abilities.

Students come with wide-ranging backgrounds, abilities, and learning styles. How can I mesh all these variables with the curriculum? The answer is found in nature. Children love to "get down and dirty" and experience nature at its finest. No one feels threatened by not knowing the correct answer or stressed about their performance. Each student can be observed without being tested. Their behavior, responses, and interaction lead me to plan their future learning experiences.

For example, hauling in buckets of dirt for a visual arts lesson can also demonstrate a science concept—what plants need to grow.

Students make dirt babies by dropping a spoonful of rye grass seed into the toe of knee-high stockings before putting in a planting medium and tying the socks off to form balls. Felt, yarn, ribbon, and foam can be used to make eyes, ears, a nose, and a mouth. The whole head is then set in a baby food jar half filled with water. The stocking becomes a wick to absorb the moisture and the seeds germinate. Wait till those dirt babies grow hair!

As you see, there is no right or wrong answer. The smartest and the slowest are on equal footing. The most studious child and the rowdiest child can both be successful. Yet I am able to answer questions such as the following: Do students work best as individuals or can they work in small groups? How do they connect prior knowledge with new information? And the list goes on.

I use several lessons about soil, worms, and seeds. Each successive lesson is a little more technical or requires more explanation or exploration from the students. This enables me to gain more insight into their abilities and learning styles. Soil is a versatile, inexpensive, and simple medium that can teach art, science, math, and social studies while reinforcing other skills.

Children are fascinated to find that Native Americans took advantage of the different hues of soil to make ceremonial paint for their faces. Indians of the Southwest used particular kinds of clay to make their pots. Today white T-shirts that have been tied and dyed in Oklahoma's red soil have created an economic boom in the tourist market. Students can examine soil with a magnifying glass or microscope to see its different components, from tiny seeds to the bodies of dead insects. They can add water to determine if the soil is mostly sand, silt, or clay based, depending on how it feels. The water-holding capacity of soil can be tested, and the students can make appropriate predictions from given patterns of evidence.

Each new lesson helps the teacher determine how to teach and what the students are going to learn. The hands-on approach makes all children active learners. Few learn by being told; most learn by doing.

Much of the Agriculture in the Classroom (AITC) material I use can be located at http://www.agclassroom.org/ok. The following are lessons I use with my dirt unit:

- Informational Skills: Build a Bug Barn, Look Out Below!
- Mathematics: Garden Grid
- Science: Case of the Missing Pumpkin, Let It Rain, Pile on the Chips, Worm Watching, Save Our Soil, Soak It Up
- Social Studies: Oklahoma Grown, Where Does the Rain Fall?
- Reading: Ride the Wild Leaf Cycle
- Visual Arts: Dirty Pictures

Helpful Tips

1. Never let the reputation precede the child.
2. Same-age, self-directed learners can be peer tutors for their classmates.
3. Older, struggling learners sometimes can provide tutoring for younger students.
4. Listen to what the children tell you about lessons. They can be good critics.
5. Have patience, patience, and more patience!
6. The core curriculum is only a basis on which to build, for both teacher and student.
7. Student ideas and thinking should help drive classroom lessons.
8. Education must be applicable to real-life problems and issues.
9. Try something new. It may be just what you need.
10. Enjoy what you do. Teaching is a calling, not just a job.

Establishing a Schoolwide Club

Christine R. Chaney
Wilmington, Delaware

After realizing that most of our students did not participate in any extracurricular activities and understanding that our school did not have the extra resources to include these kinds of activities in the learning process during the school day, I decided to implement a schoolwide club. This club would have in-school and after-school activities, correlate with the state standards for learning, and promote extracurricular activities for all of our learners.

While researching the best way to implement the club in our small school of 74 students (this year we expanded to 126 students), I happened to meet a 4-H youth development educator from the local county cooperative extension office. Through numerous discussions with her I learned about the power of 4-H and its influence on young people. As the largest informal youth educational organization in the United States, 4-H reaches more than 6.5 million children every year. Its mission is "to create supportive environments for culturally diverse youth to help them reach their fullest potential."

These clubs promote young people's growth through individual accomplishments. Through 4-H and its varied activities I could reach all learners. This was the club I was looking for, and I decided to form it as soon as possible.

First, I needed to obtain funding for all of the supplies, fees, and costs of the activities. Second, I needed to select the kinds of activities that would best reach all of our learners. Third, I had to garner the support of parents, staff, and community members. Last, the students had to be introduced to 4-H and its philosophies.

After I planned all of the activities, it was relatively easy to obtain funding from the MBNA Educational Grants program. They were excited about the establishment of a 4-H club at our school and were willing to support it financially. Funds from this institution would pay for garden supplies, arts and crafts supplies, transportation costs, and 4-H camp registration fees.

The goals for the activities were based on the interests of the students, the availability of the programs, and the Delaware State Standards of Learning. After talking with the executive director, the staff, the parents, and, most important, the students, I created a plan to incorporate a 4-H club at our school. Over a three-year period all aspects of this plan would gradually be incorporated into the regular school day, after-school hours, and Saturdays. This club would eventually influence all the students at our school.

Gathering support for 4-H activities from the executive director was effortless because he was one of its many supporters and knew it would affect all learners positively. Other members of the teaching staff were willing to include 4-H in their overall planning for the year. In fact, another teacher became my 4-H co-leader. At first, some parents and community members were willing to get involved with the preparation of some of the activities. Unfortunately, parent support waned to the point that there is only one parent who is a 4-H advisor. Community support has been easier to maintain because people in the community—especially the staff from the local cooperative extension—are interested in reaching all of our learners.

The students at our school have been the most vocal and enthusiastic supporters of 4-H. They want to participate in every activity and are constantly thinking of new ideas for the club. Without the students' support and passion for the varied activities, there would be no club.

Since I was the only leader and had a small budget, I decided to establish only two clubs with our third graders in the fall of 2001. Even though the third-grade students were the only children at the school officially enrolled in a 4-H club, the activities were open to all of our students in kindergarten through third grade. Now we have four clubs in third through fifth grade, with a total of 60 students officially enrolled in the club, and activities open to 126 students.

Each year the new club members study the 4-H pledge and its meaning, elect officers, and choose a club name. The first two years each club elected four officers, but this year we changed the election procedure. The students and I decided to combine the clubs for the election of the officers because it would be easier to coordinate the clubs' activities with four officers instead of twelve. This procedure turned into a wonderful learning experience because each club's members had to decide on a list of qualifications for each elected office: president, vice president, club reporter, and treasurer. Once the qualifications were established, each club member voted for the officers of the year's clubs.

In the spring of 2001 we were ready to begin the first 4-H activity. Since our school was located in the midst of an abandoned housing project that was soon to be demolished, I decided that we would create an oasis of gardens at our school that would be a symbol of hope for a brighter, more abundant tomorrow for the students. First, we cultivated a butterfly garden in front of the building for all to see as they entered the school. The students browsed through flower catalogs to locate flowers and plants that would attract butterflies. Several students and parents measured the small plot of grass to determine the best size for our garden. Many students participated in cultivating the yard, planting the flowers, and tending the garden. In the midst of this project several students thought of a way to brighten the front yard even more. They created a plan for making a red, white, and blue circular flower garden around the flagpole. I drove these students to the flower market so they could choose their plants. By the middle of spring our school had a flourishing butterfly and flagpole garden.

Each spring we have added to the gardens at our school. Last spring each individual classroom designed its own flower-box garden outside its window. The students helped construct the flower boxes, shovel the dirt, plant the seeds, pull the weeds, and tend to the overall care of their classroom's garden. Every child in every class was provided with hands-on experience in the aspects of creating and tending a classroom garden. The lessons involved in the formation of these gardens reached all learners because the students participated in the activities that interested them.

Our club also decided to cultivate a fruit and vegetable schoolwide garden. Each class selected fruits and vegetables to be grown in the classroom and added to the garden in late spring. The seeds were planted in the classroom, the sprouts measured, and the plants watered. Each classroom teacher planned lessons on seeds, flower gardens, and soil.

Once the fruit and vegetable garden was planted, the students had to tend to it properly for the plants to grow. This meant constant watering because the state was in a drought. The watering hose had to be connected to the indoor spigot and uncoiled outside to the gardens because we do not have an outdoor spigot. Students of all ages leaped at the chance to be the day's garden caretakers.

Our school also participated in the City of Wilmington's annual garden contests. A number of students met and greeted the judges on several Saturdays throughout the summer, to point out our gardens, explain the process of creating them, and show their enthusiasm for the gardens. That first year our 4-H club won first prize in the children's garden category, and every year after we have won second prize in the same category. Some students attend the annual ceremony to represent East Side Charter School 4-H and to receive their prize. One student told the crowd as she accepted the prize, "We work hard on our gardens."

The gardens created by the students as part of 4-H are an extraordinary example of what can happen when a project like this reaches all learners and commits them to continued beautification of their school community. Not only has each child learned important lessons about the natural world, the value of real work, and pride in his or her efforts, but also it has awakened the children's aesthetic sensibilities that will last a lifetime. As soon as we return from this year's spring break, the gardens will once again be revitalized and continue to flourish as our dedicated students tend to each garden.

The students also decided that since we have gotten more adept at planning and tending to the gardens, we need to add other particulars to our garden displays. Some of the students will construct wooden benches for people to sit on as they marvel at the flowers. Other students will build decorative birdhouses for hanging in the trees. Still others will craft and decorate wooden signs proclaiming the gardens to be the work of the East Side Charter School 4-H Club. It is amazing how the students continue to think of new and creative ideas as their interests and needs are met in the educational setting.

Another part of our 4-H plan of action is to provide the students with an opportunity to design and create an individual project for display at the Delaware State Fair each July. The first year we created thirty individual projects that won first-, second-, or third-place ribbons or participation ribbons. Last year we created sixty individual projects that won first-, second-, or third-place ribbons or participation ribbons. This year, I am proud to say, we will create seventy-five projects for display at the Delaware State Fair. This is an amazing feat considering our small staff and budget.

When the students realized they would be able to create and design a project for the state fair, they started thinking on a grand scale. One student wanted to construct a go-cart, and another wanted to build a clubhouse. While these were excellent ideas, we had to abide by the state fair project guidelines and disperse the supplies according to our budget. Still, the children thought of many unique details for their projects. Each child was able to choose a project from the following categories: woodworking, sewing, beading, drawing, latch hook, photography, and banner making.

It took several weeks in June and July to plan the projects, purchase the supplies, and find the time to work on them. Luckily I had the assistance of one of our after-care workers, who was knowledgeable in arts and crafts, to assist me the first two years. This year, however, I will have to coordinate this job by myself or procure the assistance of a community member since my assistant has moved on to another career. My determination to reach all learners is motivating me to find a solution to this particular problem, despite the overwhelming task of organizing all of these details in a couple months' time. (Our school is an eleven-month school, so we have part of the summer period to accomplish more things.)

As the students paint, draw, sew, plan, design, hammer, and varnish, I am thrilled to see each child working hard to create something of his or her own. The children use all of their unique skills to work on the project that they have chosen for the fair. They willingly give up free time during our summer camp to work on this endeavor because the children know it is something of their own that they have chosen to display to hundreds of people. While they are concentrating on some aspect of their project, you can see on their faces how much it means to them. We have many pictures of enthused, interested children as they complete the task set before them.

The first year we traveled to the state fair was an eye-opening experience for our students as they were introduced to the variety of agricultural displays in a rural setting. Most of our students are culturally and economically at risk: They live in an urban setting where many opportunities such as these are not available. As they wandered the different barns, they were awed by the birth of a cow, the speed of a horse, and the shearing of sheep. Meeting many people that day increased their awareness of the vitality of today's youth and the multicultural characteristics of today's society.

As we prepared to enter the state 4-H building, I could barely contain the students' anticipation. They were so excited about finally seeing their project on display and their awarded ribbons. The excitement was so visible that one of the 4-H workers asked me to settle the children down a little before entering. I just smiled and said they have been waiting for this moment. Every child had to show the adults where his or her project was displayed and point out the ribbon it received. The thrill of the moment became contagious as everyone around us stopped to watch our students roam the displays, searching for the project that belonged to them. This was one of the proudest moments of my educational career because I realized I had reached every learner through individual strengths and weaknesses and had assisted the students to reach their moment in the spotlight. I look forward once again this year to brilliantly showing off the talents and capabilities of our 4-H club.

Establishing a schoolwide 4-H club helped me reach many learners in ways that I never thought possible. During the day, teachers are required to teach certain lessons in a certain amount of time. These lessons don't always reach all learners, but if teachers establish a school-wide club that contains a variety of activities, teachers can reach all learners. Teachers must be willing to sacrifice much of their time for this wonderful endeavor, but it's worth it when students of all ages participate in activities that they have chosen with much enthusiasm.

Recently, our 4-H club was honored with a 2002 MBNA Best Practices in Education award. As I ponder this award, I know that I have reached all learners in a positive way, and I am more determined to continue to reach more learners as our 4-H club expands this year to include more students and activities.

Helpful Tips

1. Do extensive research on the kind of club that would be most beneficial to your students.

2. Raise money through fundraisers, letter writing, and grant applications.

3. Garner the support of parents, teachers, and community members before you form the club, so you will not be left alone in your endeavor.

4. Talk to your staff, parents, and students to find out what interests them, so you can form a club that will appeal to the students.

5. Plan, organize, and structure your day so you will have time for the club.

Using Multiple Intelligences in the Classroom

Fran Mulhern
Kennett Square, Pennsylvania

As a teacher of high school students, I have always felt concern for those students who don't succeed in the traditional way. Every year I am amazed by the nontraditional skills many of my students have. I have great artists and musicians, dancers and athletes, computer geniuses and social butterflies sitting in their seats waiting to display their talents. I believe that these great talents and resources often are unused and untapped in high school. I also strongly believe that it is these strengths that my students will use later in life to be successful. Thus I am a great believer in Howard Gardner's theory of multiple intelligences in the high school classroom.

Many eleventh graders come to me each year claiming that they are stupid and don't ever do well in social studies. I take that as a challenge to teach them how to do well and how to best comprehend material that, frankly, can be lots of fun. History is about people, and high school students are very interested in people. They spend much of their time talking about relationships and trying to understand the dynamics of relationships on many levels. My approach to teaching history is to emphasize people and people's relationships. Most of the people in history just happen to be in very important jobs and roles and end up affecting many people's lives and the outcome of history. This approach seems to bring history down to the students' level of comprehension without compromising the material. To reach their deepest levels of understanding, the material must be relevant to the students. To achieve this relevance, I tap in to their multiple-intelligence strengths.

During the first week of school, I give my students a number of surveys, including learning styles, multiple intelligences, personality temperaments, and thinking styles surveys. I compile these surveys on a spreadsheet and refer to them often so that I have a better understanding of each student in my class. I then teach my students about the theory of multiple intelligences. I explain each intelligence and tell students that everyone is smart in their own way. Unfortunately, traditional schooling focuses on only two of these eight intelligences—verbal-linguistic and logical-mathematical. Although most schools also have classes in art, music, and physical education, for my students these are all electives. I believe that these skills should be in the required subjects as well, especially if a student's intelligence strength is in one or more of these areas.

In my class, therefore, students are required to explore these intelligence strengths by creating projects that demonstrate their understanding of American history and use their intelligences. My goal is for students not only to learn history but also to learn what they are good at. At the end of each year we explore career choices based on their multiple-intelligence strengths and their personality types. They make a list of career opportunities that match their individual profiles. My hope is that they pursue careers that satisfy them, so they love what they do and are successful because they are good at what they do. I want my students to embrace each day and love going to work as I do.

For each unit of study, students are required to submit a project using one of their three top intelligence strengths. Each year I receive amazing projects. I tell them their goal is to produce a project that is so good that someone would pay money to own it. I have had many artistic students who created propaganda posters for World War I and World War II. One year I had a student create a stunning and emotionally powerful three-dimensional design of a memorial for World War II to join the other memorials in Washington, DC. The same student created a large-scale charcoal drawing of the 1920s, representing the factions of intolerance expressed during that decade. I still use it in my teaching of that concept. Two of my more musical students created a rap about the Jackson era that they then recorded in a studio. Again, I use this rap each year to teach my students this information.

This year a student created a board game on the life of Elvis Presley. I tell her frequently that she should patent it and contact a game company because it is so well prepared and fun to play. Mathematically inclined students frequently create computerized graphs to demonstrate population trends, economic trends, and timelines. I encourage students to be creative and to strive to create something unusual to express what they have learned. Their products demonstrate to me their interest in doing a good job, being creative, thinking, and having fun with the material. I truly believe that this is what learning should be about.

My message to my students is that in life they will be asked to think creatively, to come up with new ideas, and to express their knowledge in a variety of ways. Most of them will not have to take pencil-and-paper tests throughout their lifetimes but in fact will have to produce a product appropriate for use in their jobs. I believe using multiple intelligences in the classroom prepares them to think creatively and to create using new ideas. Because the brain gets bored doing the same task and using the same skills, it is essential that teachers encourage students to achieve in new ways. Making education relevant and fun is the path to achievement for students of the future.

Helpful Tips

To survey my students I use the surveys created by Dr. Thomas Armstrong. For background information I use the books by Howard Gardner at Harvard.

In my classroom I have a rainbow on one of my bulletin boards. On each color of the rainbow is one intelligence. In my teaching I stress the intelligence students are using in various activities during daily lessons and refer to the rainbow of smarts used in the real world. For instance, when I have students create skits and act them out, I explain that they are using bodily-kinesthetic skills and interpersonal skills. I try to get my students to rethink their world in school and what it means to be smart.

So much of high school is about belonging and having strong self-esteem to make good choices. I don't believe in false flattery and praise because it does not create strong self-esteem. Often the most popular or the cutest students in high school have a hard time adjusting outside of high school, where their beauty or popularity does not help them achieve. I think students should build their own strong sense of worth from within by realizing what they are good at and exploring the outer limits of what they can do.

In addition, in sharing this work with their classmates in a safe and accepting environment, students gain confidence, respect, and acceptance for their abilities. This creates an underlying sense of tolerance and acceptance in my classroom. I have little to no conflict between class members, and I believe it is because students gain an awesome respect for the talents of their classmates above and beyond taking tests and writing essays.

Reaching Special Needs Students Through a Classroom Business

Cynthia L. Pochomis
Wilmington, Delaware

Motivating my fourth-, fifth-, and sixth-grade special needs students requires a combination of patience, novel ideas, and innovative techniques. Having already faced frustration at home and within the school system, these students often lack the intrinsic desire to work hard to achieve success. To overcome this frustration, I helped them to establish Kidwormco, a student-run classroom worm business.

Kidwormco currently provides the worms for every second-grade student enrolled in a Delaware public school who uses the state-mandated soil curriculum. This business shifts the focus from learning through traditional textbook math and science instruction to learning through a real-life situation. It also provides an excellent opportunity to address the economic standards in social studies. To establish Kidwormco, the children identified a need for their product and researched and developed their product by studying the reproductive cycle and optimal growing conditions for the red worms.

On a weekly basis, those students in charge of wormery upkeep maintain an environment for reproduction by feeding, misting, and checking soil and nutrient levels. At distribution time, assembly lines are set up to most efficiently count, package, and provide a traveling environment for the worms to ensure their safe delivery.

The company treasurer and his or her staff prepare ledger sheets and billing invoices. They balance the company's checkbook and learn the value of precise bookkeeping. Each new idea is considered and tested before it is put into production, allowing the children to become decision makers and problem solvers. Our packaging, for example, is in its fourth design.

We currently charge the state of Delaware half of what the previous supplier did, while still earning a profit and saving the state about $1,000 per year. Our profits supplement classroom expenses, such as building the class library and software collections. Each worker earns a salary that is used to purchase an end-of-the-year trip. The children must determine the cost of all admissions, the bus, the meals, and souvenirs.

The purchases they make seem to have more meaning because they earned the money themselves.

The idea of establishing and running a business complete with money, dirt, and live animals is enough to turn even the most disinterested student into an inspired learner. Using math and science in real-life situations and connecting to other areas of the curriculum are key ingredients in my goal to make my students effective citizens, productive workers, knowledgeable consumers, and participants in a healthy economy.

Kidwormco is in its sixth year. Integrating math and science with economics has enabled my special needs students from diverse backgrounds to see how these subjects connect to the world in which they live. Instead of seeing math and science as separate entities, they discover them everywhere, while proving that learning and hard work can be fun.

Helpful Tips

Tips for Establishing a Classroom Business

1. Most important, identify a need in your community.

2. Team up with another enthusiastic teacher.

3. Research the product and packaging and locate suppliers.

4. Contact local businesses and corporations for mentors or donations.

5. Write grants to supplement your ideas.

6. Be flexible and retain your sense of humor.

The Use of Service Learning

Nancy B. McIver
Lincoln, New Hampshire

For the past eight years I have been using service learning as a teaching strategy, which has helped me make a significant difference in the lives of my students and in my teaching. Service learning leads to improved student learning because it provides a tremendous opportunity for teachers to connect with students.

I have also come to realize that, as a teacher, sometimes I first need to stabilize the foundation so that the structure will not collapse. This might mean meeting the physical or emotional needs of the students first, before the cognitive domain can be reached. I also believe that one of the greatest gifts we can bring to education is a sense of caring—not only caring for students but also providing students with an opportunity to care for others.

A community service learning program that my students and I developed in 1993 created a caring, respectful school environment, which supports the students as they develop positive values. The program gave us the opportunity to make connections throughout the community. My students and I created a wonderful web of intergenerational connections through our service learning experiences. The students have been most instrumental in helping the senior citizens through several outstanding initiatives, which include two publications and several projects that positively impact all the senior citizens in our community. The students have also been involved in other opportunities with children and senior citizens: helping with the Adopt a Little Friend program, working at the local community child care center, delivering meals with Meals on Wheels, visiting and helping the elderly with yard work, making quilts for the At-Risk Baby Crib Quilts program, and helping other nonprofit organizations.

One collaborative technique I use to improve student success in my classroom is grant writing. Grant writing empowers my students to determine their own path of learning. In the past eight years, most of our service learning projects have been funded with money my students received from the grants they wrote.

Because our community service learning program is so unique, we received a lot of requests to make presentations and share our information nationwide. We decided to create a resource guide detailing how to establish an intergenerational community service learning program in a high school. We needed funds to complete our work. I made several copies of a grant application and gave them to the students. The students took the application, divided the responsibilities for each section, wrote the grant, submitted it to the New Hampshire Department of Education, and were approved and received full funding for their project. They designed and developed every step of the resource guide. One student in the class had desktop publishing knowledge and took on the job of editor for the publication. Another student designed the front cover. Each of the other students completed the writing for the guide and selected poetry and photographs for the publication. They printed 1,000 copies that have been distributed nationwide. Several weeks ago I received a phone call from a woman in Virginia who found information about our resource guide on the Internet. She called to request a copy of it. We also received a request from the state of Iowa for fifty copies to be distributed to all the state's community service learning coordinators. What a compliment for the students who created the publication. Their writing was being validated and recognized by professional practitioners of community service learning throughout the country.

The students are currently working on another grant-funded program, which is a three-year project: setting up three computer sites in our community for senior citizens and citizens with disabilities. The students are currently designing the layout of the room, ordering the computer equipment and supplies, developing the computer curriculum that they will use to teach the participants, and developing survey tools to find out the needs of participants. Once the sites are established, the students will use the curriculum they developed to teach computer skills to the citizens.

Another grant-funded project students completed was a resource guide of local services for senior citizens. The students researched the much-needed information, published the educational information, and distributed the packets throughout the communities of Lincoln and Woodstock. Some of the information included how to get the senior citizen van to come to seniors' homes, how to access the Meals on Wheels program, how to get a ride to medical visits, and how to get a haircut if they are not capable of leaving their home.

Since the inception of the program, the students are viewed as active, caring, participating citizens within their community. They are finding purpose in their lives, while discovering new and positive things about themselves. Education for citizenship, through service learning, is an effective approach to bridging the gap.

Building connections is how we prevent students from dropping out of school, becoming pregnant, engaging in school violence, or committing suicide. Teachers need to make those positive connections for students, but they cannot do it alone. Teachers need the help of older community members. Every student could benefit from a senior's guidance, skill, knowledge, and unconditional love. If educators do not try to connect with all of our students, then those students who do not have a positive, guiding mentor might be influenced and accepted by individuals who do not have the students' best interests at heart. We need to provide opportunities for our students to make positive connections within the community. For society to continue, we need to care for one another. We need to build social capital by building on social relationships, which build on the capacity to be good citizens. By creating opportunities for intergenerational programs, students have the chance to gain a deeper respect for their elders and themselves. In the words of Theodore Roosevelt, "To educate a man in mind and not in morals is to educate a menace to society."

Humor in the Classroom

Marcia Wanous
Cocolalla, Idaho

Classrooms need to be places where teachers and students feel safe and respected and enjoy coming to, day after day. Setting the tone for this type of environment needs to begin on the first day of school. Teachers begin setting a tone by developing a healthy rapport with all students. Establish expectations early, model and practice, and be consistent. Try not to begin the year like a drill sergeant; instead, use humor and relax.

Look for the good in each student and use it as a hook to develop a relationship with each student. Find common interests and get to know the students. Don't be afraid to open up and share personal information. Be honest with your students and let them know when you're having a bad day or that you've made a mistake. They need to see teachers are human, too.

I have tried many different techniques throughout my twenty-four years of teaching; through trial and error and training in the Love and Logic program I have developed what I consider to be a good environment in my classroom.

I love using humor in my classroom to get the students off guard and relaxed. I still need to discipline, but I am able to use humor with it. Just recently I had a student who was getting ready to go to physical education class. I noticed as he was heading out the door that he had a stuffed bunny in his hands. He was awfully proud of that bunny, but I knew it would not be allowed in the gym. Rather than tell him he couldn't take the bunny with him, I told him that the bunny couldn't go because it didn't have its tennis shoes. He thought that was pretty funny, but he knew that I meant no toys allowed, and he put it away. Instead of me dictating orders, we had a little fun, and I got the same results with a better attitude.

When a student is busy playing with a pencil, rolling it back and forth on the desk and driving me crazy, I put my focus on the pencil. I might say, "Chris, your pencil is really hyperactive today. I don't think it is paying attention. What do you think? Should we put it in time out or give it a second chance?"

I had another student who was constantly in motion when we met at the carpet for lessons. It was normal for him to try out several different spots in one lesson. One day he was particularly busy, to the point of even lying on his back and stretching his foot in the air. Without hesitating, I grabbed his foot and put my face very close to it and gave it a lecture. I told it, "You need to sit down and pay attention. You're driving me crazy!" Everyone had a good laugh, including the child, and he sat up and joined us as I continued the lesson.

I use humor on the playground as well, and it seems to ease the tension and get the students off guard a little. There are swings that "throw" kids out, slides that "talk" kids into sliding down headfirst, balls that "jump" on the roof, and toys that "won't share."

My philosophy is to have fun and make sure the students are having a good time, too. I try not to let the little things get to me. It's a challenge I look forward to every day.

Helpful Tips

A wonderful resource for any classroom teacher or parent is *Discipline With Love and Logic.* The authors, Jim Fay and Foster Cline, are experts in the area of humor and discipline. For more information, visit the Love and Logic Web site (www. loveandlogic.com).

Life's Unnerving Little Habits

Brandy Fenenga
Watertown, South Dakota

Tap. Tap. Tap. The constant pencil tapping was starting to get on my nerves, and it was only the beginning of the class. Pencil tapping seemed to be one of Chris's nervous little habits. Granted, lots of people tap their pencils on the desk while they are thinking, but this went far beyond that. This had come to be a major distraction—not only for me but for all the other students in the class as well. Chris had several nervous habits; pencil tapping was only one of many. I often wondered if he would be bald by the time he graduated high school because another habit of his was pulling his hair out when frustrated— clumps of it by the fistful. He also had a tendency to sigh very loudly whenever frustrated, which was quite often. Chris had been diagnosed with Asperger syndrome after suffering through an ineffective treatment as a result of an incorrect diagnosis. Chris was a fifteen-year-old with raging hormones, capable of doing the work of a high school freshman but with the emotional maturity of only a third grader (and that was on a good day).

This conflict had resulted in several meltdowns over the school year; he just couldn't deal with something when he had to work very hard at it. The nervous habits as well as the occasional meltdowns had become major distractions for the other students and caused teachers to almost live in fear. Chris honestly didn't realize that he was pulling big clumps of hair out of his head or driving everyone to the brink of insanity with the constant, loud pencil tapping. If I said anything to him, it didn't help the situation much because he didn't realize that the behavior was happening—hard to control something when you don't know you are doing it. He would apologize but would be back to the same behavior in fewer than two minutes.

We tried a stress ball first. This worked a little, but he would forget to bring it to class and had to go get it. The other students wanted one, too, and got just as distracted when he was using the stress ball, even though it was quieter than the pencil tapping. Ultimately, the stress ball suffered a similar fate as his hair, totally shredded within about two weeks. What was needed was something to distract him to keep him from pulling his hair or tapping his pencil, but it had to be something that wouldn't distract the rest of the class. His hair and pencil were easily accessible, so the substitute had to be something that was within immediate reach. What resulted was a piece of fish tubing, tied first to the end of his pencil and then in a big knot at the end. The purpose of the knot at the end was to give him something to chew on instead of tapping the pencil or pulling the hair. An unorthodox solution, but it seemed to work. At first, I had to remind him of the behavior by simply saying his name. Then he remembered that he was supposed to chew on the tubing. The knot at the end was a little large, so if he did start tapping, the pencil would be off balance enough to alert him to the behavior (it was also quieter).

After several days, he automatically started to chew on the end of the tubing instead of tapping the pencil. Several weeks went by, and I noticed that he didn't chew on the pencil as much either. The chewing seemed to calm him better than the other habits. Just as many babies outgrow a pacifier on their own, the same thing happened with the fish tubing. Chris outgrew his dependence on the fish tubing on his own by the end of the year. The following year, teachers rarely saw pencil tapping or hair pulling.

Helpful Tips

A substitute for a bad habit must be something quiet but not something that the other students will be interested in. It should also be something the teacher and classmates can live with.

(Continued)

Chris also started answering questions verbally when he became frustrated with short-answer or essay questions on assignments or tests. These types of assignments posed difficulty because they require a certain amount of sequencing before writing. Chris knew the answer to the question, but his brain was unable to process it in the right order—he would focus so much on what to write first that he was unable to write anything at all. By giving Chris the option of answering verbally, he could tell the teacher what he was trying to write and the teacher would write it as he said it, without offering any other forms of help.

 ## Using Affinity Groups to Promote Professional Development and Enhance School Climate

Susan Okeson
Anchorage, Alaska

Get the setting—the teachers' turf—right . . . and the chances for good schooling will improve.

Barth (1990, p. xi)

An affinity group is simply a group with a common interest or characteristic. At Wonder Park elementary we built our school improvement plan on the premise that when people become aware of commonalities between them, their work will be better and their relationships will be stronger.[1] This simple premise—of discovering ways to find commonalities among people—has proved to be one of the strongest, most productive ways to inject renewal and energy into a school's intellectual and social environments. Using affinity groups is not particularly difficult, yet the rewards are incalculable.[2] The basic outline and intellectual framework behind affinity groups is shared later in this section, but, in the final analysis, all school improvement plans will depend on how much people believe in the project and how convincing the school's leader is. I can provide some notes, but the true melody of school improvement is achieved only if the principal can orchestrate the disparate players of any school staff in a harmonious way. Affinity groups have been the best way that I have seen to bring so many different drummers together.[3]

Step 1: Professional Study Groups

First, I believe that the technique our school employed in using affinity groups to establish professional study groups was more important than the topics of study.[4] In other words, it was not great topics but great cohesiveness that became the common denominator for success. The staff at my school put people together using the affinity group concept and therefore defeated the usual staff groupings of grade level, teaching proximity, and previous connections.

Here is how our staff got started: At a staff meeting, teachers hung about fifty pieces of chart paper along the walls. They then invited everybody to start listing topics worthy of a study group, writing only one idea on each piece of paper. People could write as many ideas as they liked, and they could use other people's written ideas to sharpen a focus or change directions. The key was to have more sheets of paper hanging around the room than the staff could fill out in their allotted time. It took about fifteen minutes to write ideas, browse the room, and put topics on most of the sheets of paper.

This was a no-talking exercise. The rationale behind the no-talking rule was to foster serious thought and lessen the likelihood of distractive factions traveling in packs. Then the teachers regrouped and were told to take a tour of the entire room and sign up for the one topic that they would like to spend the year pursuing in their professional study group—again, with the no-talk rule in effect.

Study Group Components

Mandating silence, using staff creativity, and displaying ideas on chart paper may not eliminate teacher cliques entirely, but it makes them much less likely. The wall chart topics ranged from studying brain research, getting parents involved, using technology, employing early-reading strategies, using learning rewards, fostering school climate, and improving customer service. Getting different people together around a common interest instantly makes them an affinity group. These groups expanded the relationships in the building and eliminated the resistance that often accompanies top-down, principal-chosen topics. Group members had immediate buy-in to the topic and a shared sense of value with group members because, of all the groups they could have joined, they selected this one, these people. Now the success or failure of a group's work could not be placed outside the affinity group.

These affinity groups met bimonthly, had to select a book on their topic to read together, kept journal notes, and made sharing presentations to the staff.[5] The sharing presentation was to model good teaching, generate enthusiasm, use technology and visual learning components, and be incredibly clear. Each affinity group's goal was to make a convincing case for their topic's significance and break it down into digestible kernels that could be understood and used in their colleagues' classes immediately. Using affinity groups for professional development like this led to some very readily recognizable results. First, new connections between often-separated staff members occurred. Second, research methods were shared, and these methods unearthed some very sophisticated data, which empowered trust and brought legitimacy to the groups and direction to the school itself. The feeling of being part of something significant, worthwhile, and important was unmistakable. And, perhaps most impressive, the entire staff witnessed many first-rate examples of good teaching via the affinity groups' presentations. This peer modeling of good teaching was an excellent way to showcase the different ways fellow professionals impart information.

Ground Rules

Our overarching rule in the staff affinity groups was that teachers must care more about the people they were studying with than the subject they were studying. The product of a group's research must never be paid for with the currency of our professional relationships. Leaders made everyone promise that congenial relationships would rank higher than the project. And it was a requirement that everyone must have fun. Leaders promoted enjoyment and established that boredom was always a self-inflicted choice. Teachers strictly ascribed to the adage that we can take our work seriously but not ourselves and that people's respect, treatment, and dignity will win out every time in a dispute over content or presentation.

Step 2: Student Affinity Groups

Student affinity groups were a natural by-product of the staff working together, and the potential for student recognition is as limitless as a leadership team's imagination. Teachers were so pleased with the adult dividends that were paid from investing their efforts in commonality among the staff that they decided to diversify their investment to students. The premise and mission were as follows: If we create commonality among students, we improve school climate.

If people have something in common with each other, they are much more likely to be kind to each other. This philosophy means using affinity groups as both a way to improve school climate and decrease harassment and a way to increase civility and decrease hostility. So our school went looking for commonalities and found that there are millions.

A simple place to start was with a name twins board. A name twins board is a collage of all students with the same name, for example, all students named Mary on one poster board. A digital camera and some creative artwork trim the poster and form a student-centered bridge builder. Students love seeing themselves in print, and they get to know others who were before just faces in the school crowd, invisible faces in different grades.

A birthday board is another effective way to find connections and put students in positive contact with each other. Some mornings the teachers ask for everyone with a black lab for a pet to come to the office. A staff member takes a picture, makes a poster, and adorns our walls with student faces and common bonds. What is fun about student affinity groups is that teachers can get as creative as they wish, and they can hang such displays all over the building. Parents love seeing student pictures displayed around the school, and staff pictures are mixed in with student affinity groups everywhere. Middle-name twins, red-hair twins, homes with gerbils, students with relatives in Michigan, or any quirky combination under the sun are all fair game.

In the Final Analysis

In the end, affinity groups bring people together and produce better work and friendlier environments. Whether used as a staff development tool or a student climate builder, affinity groups may be the most exciting single aspect in elementary education today.[6] In short, our staff members firmly believe that it is the relationships of a school that determine that school's success. If I have learned anything over the years, it is that a successful school cannot result from canned programs or cut-and-paste curriculum; behind every great school is a community of professionals who support each other first. Or, as Routman (1996) states, "Programs don't teach; teachers do" (p. 126). Teachers put their time into good relationships, and good work is a natural by-product.

Measurability

Let me say that most of my favorite professional practices cannot be measured well. Some of the most effective practices are the least measurable, and the affinity group concept is no different. However, our school did raise student test scores. I believe that our collegiality is the sole reason that our test scores have consistently improved, but researchers would cringe at such an antimeasurability stance. That's okay. I'll leave it to the researchers to quantify data and search for causation; we'll spend our time supporting each other and celebrating our successes.

Notes

1. School improvement plan is used here as a self-appointed, site-based effort to improve. We analyze our school goals periodically throughout the year for assessment and adjustment.

2. Much of this article is based upon premises detailed in Roland Barth's seminal book, *Improving Schools From Within*. Our plan is merely an extension of the wonderful foundation professor Barth has provided. I would suggest this text as a faculty read and the critical first step to any school improvement plan.

3. Although not the subject of this article, the art of the principalship is ultimately defined through his/her ability to inspire and be convincing to an over-worked, under-appreciated work force—a Promethean challenge.

4. You will hear repeatedly in this article how a good process led to better content. This is one of our marks of uniqueness, in keeping with Roland Barth, that when relationships are fostered good work will follow.

5. The affinity groups' expectations were established jointly by the groups themselves. After we gathered by affinity groups, we collectively detailed how we would document, assess, and present our findings in creative, interesting ways.

6. This is not to say that such activities would not work at the secondary level, for they certainly would. Most of my experience is at the elementary level, but minor adaptations upon this model could surely improve even the collegiate environment.

References

Barth, R. (1990). *Improving schools from within.* San Francisco: Jossey-Bass.
Routman, R. (1996). *Literacy at the crossroads.* Portsmouth, NH: Heinemann.

Raising Citizens

Deni Lynn Lopez
Simi Valley, California

Thirty students anxiously awaited the arrival of the train, signaling the start of their three-day trip to Sacramento, California. They boarded the Coast Starlight at 10:20 A.M. on Wednesday, May 20th, at the Simi Valley Amtrak station. As they traveled up the coast, the students marveled at the oceans, pastures, and other sights out their windows. They compared what they expected to see at the different stops to what they actually encountered. Their observations were recorded in a journal to be later turned into a travel brochure.

The students were active participants on this journey; indeed they had become experts on all aspects of the trip. They had calculated transportation, housing, and food costs; planned the scheduled activities; researched what they would see on the train and at the city; and made contacts with state legislators in Sacramento. To help raise money for student scholarships they sold candy, ran a holiday boutique, held a rummage sale, and organized a jogathon. The class developed bookkeeping skills while keeping track of inventory and profits. They learned to read a city map and detailed directions to various places in

Sacramento. The students were able to interpret the complicated train schedule while researching what their journey up the coast would be like. They wrote to California's Department of State Parks to get information about the various museums they could visit. This information was used to make oral presentations about what the students could see in Sacramento.

Once in Sacramento, groups of students proudly showed off the museums they had researched weeks before the trip. On the first day in Sacramento they visited the governor's mansion, Sutter's Fort, the Railroad Museum, the Eagle Theater, and Whitter Ranch. Each stop was like its own field trip with the opportunity to apply an earlier learned language arts or math skill. Whitter Ranch, where they experienced life on a farm in the early 1900s, was a favorite stop. Here they were able to pet farm animals; make a dinner from scratch, consisting of biscuits, butter, salad, stew, lemonade, and ice cream; and make corn husk dolls and other crafts. By the time they got back to the hotel at 9:30 P.M., they were tired and ready for bed.

The next day they toured the state capitol and visited Coloma's Gold Country. The students got a standard tour of the capitol, where they learned how a bill becomes a law; saw the rooms where each of the legislative branches meet; and looked at the county showcases. Then they boarded the bus for the 1.5-hour ride into the hills outside of Sacramento to visit Coloma's Gold Discovery Park. Here they climbed rocks, walked through old mining buildings, hiked the trails, and panned for real gold. Finally, with the second day in Sacramento coming to an end, they boarded the plane to fly home at around 9:00 A.M the next morning.

This was more than the usual class field trip to the state capitol. By researching and making all the reservations I was able to offer this trip to my students and their parents for only $180.00 per person. I used the planning aspects of the trip as a vehicle to educate and motivate my students. Participation in all aspects of this trip created ownership as well as a reason to learn. The students were empowered with the knowledge that they could participate in the world around them in a positive manner. This was just one example of the outstanding learning experiences and adventure my students encounter.

The projects and activities the students are involved in are more than just exciting activities. My belief that students learn best when they are involved in authentic tasks that enable them to acquire and apply basic skills in meaningful ways is the driving force behind my unit selection. Other examples of learning projects my students are involved in include the design and construction of a one-quarter-acre garden for the school campus, the creation and management of the Garden Store, and the operation of a schoolwide paper mill.

In addition, by writing and publishing a how-to garden book, as well as other important informational material for distribution to the public, the students have developed effective communication skills. While students enjoy the educational adventures they are involved in, the stage is set for a high level of student achievement. By aligning units of study with grade-level standards, I maintain a high level of integrity that provides me with the rationale for the projects I choose and the confidence that my students are establishing the foundations for skills they will need in the next grade level. In addition to motivating students, lessons are specifically designed to address the varying needs and abilities of the students. To meet the language development, resource, Title 1, GATE, and regular students' needs, I regularly run three reading groups, four writing groups, two math groups, and various cooperative groups throughout the day. The culture of the classroom reflects a community in which individuals act responsibly, feel free to take risks, and work toward a common goal.

I recently moved the focus of my instruction to environmental education issues. This year's students have worked hard to save their school's quarter-acre garden, create a bird habitat, run the worm farm, and recycle the school's wastepaper, while educating students, staff members, and school board members on the importance of recycling.

The weed-infested school garden was slowly dying from apathy and disuse when the students decided to get involved. For help with mowing and cleaning, they sent out flyers for monthly Saturday garden workdays, resulting in more than 250 volunteer hours being contributed. Through grants, recycling drives, and cheesecake sales, the students have raised money for trees, bushes, and flowers to replace the defiant crabgrass. Students researched which plants would attract birds and butterflies, called nurseries to get the best prices, designed possible native plant gardens, and ultimately planted fourteen trees and hundreds of plants to bring beauty and life back into the garden.

To encourage other teachers to support the garden, the students researched fun, quick garden activities that they could teach other students during recess. Then, with the help of yard duty, they opened the garden up during recess for primary students' enjoyment. Some of the activities they taught students were how to dry flowers, make grassheads, and create garden masks.

In addition to saving the school garden, the students independently ran the school worm farm, collected the school's wastepaper for recycling, ran schoolwide contests to encourage more recycling, and educated the school on vermin composting. Once the students taught our school how important recycling is for the environment, they set their eyes on educating other schools. They wrote letters and spoke before the school board, requesting the adoption of a districtwide recycling program that would encourage other schools to limit their paperwaste output through recycling. Finally, students are designing a Web page that documents how they run the worm farm and organize the recycling program, so other schools can follow their program.

This project was integrated throughout the curriculum and provided students the vehicle by which to learn and apply almost all of the required fifth-grade standards in math, reading, writing, and listening and speaking.

The goal of this project was to couple environmental education with grade-level standards to dramatically reduce the trash schools throw away and create environmentally responsible students. The project's environmental goals were to continue to reduce the amount of trash our school produces, to educate other students and our community on the importance of recycling, and to keep our quarter-acre garden from being abandoned. The educational goals of the project were to provide an opportunity for students to learn and apply grade-level standards through real-life projects. The ultimate goal of the project was to transform students into citizens who care about the environment around them, understand their responsibility to protect it, and are empowered with the knowledge that they can make a difference.

As a humanitarian my goal was to inspire children to care about the environment and empower them with the knowledge that they can make a difference if they choose to. As a teacher my goal was to provide a vehicle to teach grade-level standards and motivate students to do their personal best. The following is part of the speech I gave at the National Agriculture in the Classroom Conference:

> Sixty-five percent of our students are at risk. The question then becomes how can we better serve these students? Brain research tells us the brain learns best when it sees a reason to learn. While we teachers may think raising test scores is important, I haven't found better test scores in May to be real motivating factors for fourth and fifth graders in October.
>
> Coupling standards-based instruction with service learning creates a win-win situation in this current "raise test scores" educational setting. In this format (coupling standards-based instruction with service learning), an agricultural lesson doesn't take away from math time. Determining profits from a garden store becomes the math lesson. Writing a how-to garden book can be part of a reading program as students are motivated to revise their written work until their piece is ready for publication.
>
> In addition, I chose to teach via garden-based service projects because I am an environmentalist—not a tree hugging environmentalist, just someone who cares about the earth. I feel it is my duty as an educator to teach my students how to be responsible citizens who are conscious of their impact on the earth and empowered with the knowledge that they can make a difference in the world around them.
>
> Here are the words my fifth graders wrote in their reflective journals in response to the question, why do we run the worm farm:

> We have a worm farm because we care about the environment.
>
> *Cristal*

> We are in charge of it because we're the ones who wanted the job and we're the ones who want to help the earth.
>
> *Chloe*

We have the worm farm so landfills will stay small. I'm in charge of the worm farm because no other class will do it.

Maia

We have a worm farm for mainly one reason. Our worm farm eats most of the food that would have been thrown away and filled up another landfill.

Ashley

We have a worm farm to save landfills and keep the earth clean. We are in charge because we are the only ones who care. I feel good because it means that Mrs. Lopez thinks we are responsible.

Michael

We have a worm farm because the food that we collect doesn't go to waste. We are in charge of running it because we wanted to do it. I feel very good about running the worm farm because it is fun and we're helping the environment.

Joel

When we have higher test scores as our goal, standards-based instruction, may give us more students who can raise their test scores five to ten points. But what else can they do?

When real-life learning becomes the goal of standards-based instruction, we produce students who have endless possibilities in what they can do, and we get higher test scores in the process. If I am going to send a message through children, I don't want to send the message that this is how you pass the test, this is how you answer the question. I want them to learn to read to understand things, write to be able to express themselves, use math to solve problems. I want them to take responsibility for their lives and the world around them.

◨ Weekly Reflections

Wendy Miller
Cove City, North Carolina

Weekly "Reflections"

Rubric Point Totals

Name: _____

Week of: _____

Monday: _____

Tuesday: _____

Wednesday: _____

Thursday: _____

Friday: _____

Total Points: _____

Point Goal: _____

Circle yes or no:

I met my weekly goal.   YES   NO

My Daily Rubric

Wendy Miller
Cove City, North Carolina

My Daily Rubric

Mrs. Miller's Class

"BE THE BEST YOU CAN BE!!!"

Name: _____   Teacher: Mrs. Miller

Date: _____   My Point Goal for the Week: _____   **Bonus: _____

	Criteria				Points
	3	*2*	*1*	*0*	
I will come to school on time each day.	I was unpacked and in my seat when the tardy bell rang!!	I was still unpacking or out of my seat when the tardy bell rang.	I came to school between 8:30 and 10:00.	I came to school after 10:00.	____
I will come to school prepared to work.	I have all my supplies today!!	I came to school without 1 of my supplies.	I came to school without 2 of my supplies.	I came to school without 3 or more supplies.	____
I will complete my homework each night.	I returned my homework folder with ALL my work complete!!	I returned my homework folder with most of my work complete.	I returned my homework folder with more than ½ of my work complete.	I did not return my homework folder.	____
I will complete my class work each day.	I earned 6 stars today!!	I earned 4-5 stars.	I earned 2-3 stars.	I earned less than 2 stars.	____
I will follow the classroom rules I helped create.	I have no sticks in my bus seat!!	I have 1-2 sticks in my bus seat.	I had 3-4 sticks in my bus seat.	I have more than 5 sticks in my bus seat.	____
				Total →	

Student Reflection: _____

_____

Teacher Comment/Signature: _____

_____

Parent Comment/Signature: _____

_____

*__**Bonus: +1 for returning your Rubric signed by your parent.__*

CHAPTER *7*

Reaching All Learners With Social Studies

 Differentiated Instruction to Reach All Learners: Geography

Lynn Williams
Lafayette, Colorado

In 2001, the Boulder Valley School District adopted a new social studies curriculum for all grade levels. The kindergarten classrooms were to implement the continents of Africa and Antarctica by the 2002–2003 school year.

The abstract idea of continents for a kindergartener was far beyond the reach for our diverse second-language population. With a few other kindergarten teachers from the district our kindergarten team attempted to take this abstract idea and have it become a tangible one. We decided to develop a hands-on curriculum for our native English and second-language learners. My pedagogical background is Montessori, so implementing this type of differentiated learning to meet all learners was something I found to be practical and fun.

I began my unit with the study of the world, using a globe and a wonderful Montessori wooden world map. The children were introduced to a seven continents song in relation to their placement on the map. They were then presented with a timeline of activities in conjunction with the map work: reproducing the world map with watercolors and using felt pieces to make the continents of the world.

Books about Antarctica were then created. The students were able to view many photographs of the continent. While the children looked at these photographs, I asked, "What does this photograph of Antarctica tell you?" The children's responses ranged from "It is cold" to "It is white" to "It has penguins." After developing this background knowledge I presented the enlarged continent of Antarctica. I made a fabric replica of the continent with white fur and also made a three-dimensional model of the Transatlantic Mountains. We then began our research on the habitat of Antarctica. We measured ourselves in comparison with the emperor penguin, we counted penguins by tens, and we created stamp work of animal life in Antarctica. The final culminating event was the penguin backpack that was sent home with one child for a week. Inside the penguin backpack were several books on Antarctica, stuffed penguins, supplies for writing a story about penguins, and a penguin book, in which the children were to write their own personal story. The Antarctica unit was completed in January.

Then we began studying Africa. The study of this continent lasted until May. We begin the continent of Africa in much the same way we did Antarctica. We used the felt piece of Africa, which defined the desert regions, the Nile River, Lake Victoria, the grasslands, and the rainforest regions. Due to the vastness of this continent we chose only two countries to explore. (Each year my class varies in which countries it chooses to study.) After selecting countries, the students began studying the Masai tribes, gradually building their background knowledge of these people, and eventually they learned about the African hut.

The African hut began its formation with a simple wooden frame. Next we placed cardboard around the hut, and then we attached reddish-brown butcher paper over the structure. Finally, using mud, we created the claylike effect. The roof was assembled with raffia and more butcher paper. We then finished our KWL (what we KNOW, what we WANT to know, and what we LEARNED) chart about the Masai people and created rules for behavior in the hut. Then I opened the hut for a choice activity. Children experienced wearing Masai clothes, getting sand on their toes, hearing music from the region, playing musical instruments, and reading numerous books in the mosquito-netted reading corner.

I cross the curriculum in the Africa unit by writing and reading throughout the day. While some children experienced the hut, others worked on a writing activity about the continent of Africa, while using *National Geographic* photos as a research tool. Other activities, such as the following, are also available:

- Counting African beads by tens
- Counting using African-animal stamps
- Creating an African weaving
- Matching African-animal mothers and their babies by matching the footprints of plastic animals
- Tracing the continent of Africa and then using a fine motor tool to poke out the continent
- Making a book with African pictures inside
- Creating spots or stripes animal art projects

In the kindergarten art class we furthered our research on Africa by incorporating the book *The Colors of Kenya,* by Fran Sammis (1998). I cut out templates for each color represented in the book. For example, the color red (*nyekundu*) represents the Masai tribe. I then cut out varying hues of black and brown and had the children place red fabric and paper on the templates that represent the Masai people. We then took oil pastels and created the jewelry and red mud that is smeared on the heads of the Masai women. I continued this artwork with the color green (*kijani kibichi*), which represents the coffee bean plantations; pink (*waridi*), which identifies the flamingos; and with the color gray (*kijivu*), which represents the baobab tree and the elephant, the most exciting for the children. This year we will also make zebra or cheetah masks, finger pianos, and dolls.

Our final project in art was the creation of Kente cloths, which the children wore as their own personalized costume for the music production at the end of the year. We received a grant this year to provide Kindermusik to our children. The children will receive a few lessons on

African musical instruments and song. Throughout our unit on Africa we also studied foods of the region during snack time, created a marketplace with trading beads, and held lively discussions about anything that came up during our study of Africa.

This total immersion in the social studies curriculum proved to be beneficial and has continued to be so year after year. All of the children at our school, whatever their first language, know the continents through song by the end of their kindergarten year.

Children are naturally inquisitive about the exotic animals of Antarctica and Africa. By creating an environment with hands-on activities, I enhanced their learning of a very abstract idea.

Reference

Sammis, F. (1998). *Colors of Kenya.* Minneapolis, MN: Lerner.

Research-Based Teaching Practices to Reach All Learners

Marc Stanke
Brookfield, Wisconsin

I have had the pleasure to teach twelfth-grade economics and honors economics for my entire career. Even though Wisconsin does not require economics for graduation, nearly two-thirds of the high schools in Wisconsin require it. Every school I have taught in requires it for graduation. As one can imagine, not every high school student is thrilled at the prospect of learning supply and demand mechanics, tax theory and application, personal finance, market structure and competition, and the not-so-exciting gross domestic product topic. Early in my career, I realized that I needed to generate the same level of passion I felt for economics in my students. Constructivist learning emphasizes the building of scaffolding, in which students can, from a present, cognitive structure, expand their knowledge and comprehension. Teachers also know that student learning occurs when students feels good about themselves and the environment in which they learn. I also take into consideration that kinesthetic learning can lead to greater abstract learning. My method of teaching economics is to make the topic seem less theoretical by using drama, simulations, crazy anecdotes, and games that allow the students to create a scaffolding of memories to which they can attach meaning.

For example, when I introduce the abstract concepts of demand and supply, I use the history of the hula hoop to introduce the changes in demand, supply, and the increases and decreases in price. I take the students into the past, and we pretend the year is 1958, the year Richard Knerr and Arthur "Spud" Melin invented the hula hoop. The students are hired to market and sell the product in class. The students start spinning the hoops and using them for all sorts of things. What is amazing is that the students do not know the history, but their logic allows them to recreate why the demand increased and how the price reacted. It allows them to predict why the founders of the hoop could not get a patent and how that led to an increase in copycat hoops.

They can predict that product differentiation would occur to increase or revive the demand and make the price increase. During this time, the students enjoy trying to hula hoop and convince others to buy it. This entertaining and fun strategy allows everyone to have a good time, predict outcomes, understand how prices are formed and then change in a market economy, and predict how others will react. During the rest of the unit, when a student struggles with the abstract concept, all I need to do is take the student back to the hoop activity and remind him or her of the event. The student then takes what he or she learned in the activity and generalizes it to an abstract concept.

Another activity I use to help all learners feel a part of the class, while using experiential learning to simplify abstractions, is a game of musical unemployment chairs. I use this to demonstrate the six causes of unemployment. Ten to fifteen students form a circle and occupy a chair, like in the child's game of musical chairs. However, in this game each chair represents a full-time job with great benefits. There is no unemployment compensation or welfare system in my class, called Stankeland. When the music stops, the student must find and occupy a chair. I manipulate the chairs by removing them or replacing a chair with a smaller chair, a computer, or a piece of machinery as the game progresses. The kids love it because they are competitive and want a chair (job). The removal of chairs or replacement with other objects allows them to form a permanent image of the cause of unemployment, and it leads to a springboard effect of additional questions.

I use the actual vocabulary during the synthesis questions at each phase. The students are all actively involved, and I question the students affected by a change as to the reason for their emotions. The students enjoy coming to class, and they realize it will be activity based. They form memories to which they can attach meaning. All students are successful, so it eliminates feelings of inadequacy. Many students are in the class because it's required, but I want them to enjoy the experience. People tend to experience deeper learning in courses they enjoy and value.

 ## Differentiated Instruction to Reach All Learners: Economics

Marc Stanke
Brookfield, Wisconsin

My school lists differentiation of instruction as one of its goals. All students have unique abilities and interest levels. For that reason, teachers need to instruct students as individuals, not as widgets in a factory assembly process. In my economics classes, I use differentiation in several ways. I have taught for seventeen years, so I can sense which topics will be more difficult for various learners. The expectations I have for my students are extraordinarily high. I believe when teachers set the bar high, provide students with enough opportunities to clear the bar, and provide various methods to learn how to clear the bar, students will meet and often exceed the expectations.

When I prepare a lesson, I consider the outcomes I want students to demonstrate. Next I consider the assessment I might use to evaluate their learning. Third, I consider whether the curriculum is adequate to meet that outcome or if I need to develop more materials. Finally, I choose the instructional strategies I will use. Almost every major unit has an assessment. I provide students with a list of items they can select from to demonstrate their learning. Some lists might include assessments such as a test, a fishbowl debate, a speech, a poster, a PowerPoint presentation, a poem, an anthology of related articles, or a group activity.

I encourage my students to develop their own assessment. Often they prefer to select, but during the process they add wrinkles and twists that make it more elaborate. I use quizzes to assess understanding of learning in small segments, such as weekly. In addition, when I plan instruction, I consider the needs and abilities of each class. One of my classes is operating at a higher level, and they require more problem-solving activities to apply, evaluate, and synthesize their knowledge. Some students might require more comprehension activities, so I might ask them to make a graphic organizer, using Inspiration software, to link the concepts. Students might play economics Jeopardy to test their knowledge of terms and give students the opportunity to write and answer five questions. I try to conference with all of my students, and, if I feel one or two students might benefit from cooperative learning, I plan an activity where they are in a mixed-ability group.

Differentiating instruction is more difficult in classes where there are thirty or more students. I have found that if I spend more time planning the lesson, allowing the outcomes and assessments to drive my instructional strategies, more students are reached. There is a saying that typifies older instructional strategies: "Are you the sage on the stage or the guide on the side?" I prefer to be the guide on the side because I can differentiate the delivery of content better. Students who seem to be more artistic are encouraged to use this ability to demonstrate learning artistically. Some students are more analytical, and they might prefer to be evaluated using a numerical and logical approach. My goal as a teacher is to get them to use all of their intelligences and to grow as learners in all of these areas.

I am not a strong believer in the use of like-ability groups. Society does not arrange itself intentionally this way, and, if democracy is expected to flourish (the chief goal of social studies education), we must all function effectively together. Many economics courses are taught as a problem-solving and real-life application process. If students cannot use a theory and apply it (even in a rudimentary form), what is the value of asking them to learn it? Because in social studies we are all expected to understand the issues, discuss them, persuade each other, arrive at a decision, and ultimately vote, then I believe we should learn the concepts and practice them in a classroom that consists of students at all ability levels. My own anecdotal conclusions are that lower ability students perform better and learn more in a class of their peers—students at all levels—rather than in a modified class consisting of entirely lower ability students. I am not a special education teacher, and some of my philosophy might be due to my own lack of preparedness to instruct special learning students best.

🐚 Engaging All Students in Social Studies

Denise L. Carlson
Gilbert, Iowa

Students in today's schools are often identified by what goals they've met, what their standardized test scores are, and what they can and can't do. While I believe that assessment plays an important role in instruction, it is not the only piece to the puzzle. Defining a child solely by test scores rubs me the wrong way. In my mind, the perfect school would believe that all children can learn—perhaps at varying degrees of mastery, but learn nonetheless. Therefore, rather than merely raising the bar and commanding students to jump over it, educators need to search for students' unique learning styles, connect new learning to schema they've already developed, fill their classrooms with laughter and emotion, and, above all else, make learning personal and engaging.

As a public school student, many years ago, I rarely felt the personalness of learning. Rather, I recall wondering, "What has this got to do with me? Why is this important?" I was especially dumbfounded by the dates, names, and places in social studies classes. I always wished that this ancient history I was reading about had some connection to my real life. So, when I became a teacher, I vowed that learning would not be boring. I decided to try to make lessons fun, engaging, and meaningful. It is this personal promise that led me to collaborate with a fellow teacher to revamp our social studies curriculum.

When we began, we realized that major publishing houses usually focused on communities in third-grade materials. But these books seemed cumbersome, uninviting, and one-dimensional to us. They did not have the personal-engagement factor that seemed necessary to get nine-year-olds excited about social studies. We felt it was essential to connect students to the concept of community and history, rather than have them simply read about it. We also knew that to understand communities and cultures outside of central Iowa, our students would need a personal understanding of their own family community and personal history. With this belief we created our first unit of study. In this unit, through a variety of activities, the children discovered that history is not just a list of dates and places; rather, history is a personal thing.

The first social studies lesson of the year is to research first names. The children are anxious to interview their parents and discover why their own name was selected. Through class discussion and a concept attainment framework, children discover that there are four main reasons why birth names are selected. Some students are named after family members; some are named after famous people. Some children are given Biblical names, and other names are chosen just because Mom and Dad like them. Next, via the Internet, the students further research their name and discover its meaning and place of origin. This leads to their first ah-ha moment, when they realize that their name was influenced by a culture far removed from Iowa.

Further activities include comparing and contrasting community traditions by compiling a book of treasured family recipes and the stories that go along with them. Every family community, just like city or national communities, develops their own time-honored traditions. Families quite often exemplify their traditions during holidays. This becomes clear to children when they hear family stories and sample traditional foods.

Next we explore how communities have unique laws and routines. This is done when each child reports on their wake-up time, bedtime, and homework time in their family community. Once again we compile an inclusive class list and use computer technology to create graphs and charts that depict our learning. By looking at graphs, the children can see commonalities in family routines while simultaneously viewing that there are many versions of acceptable routines.

Finally, the children discover that all communities have valued possessions. This is accomplished when each child makes a memory box and inserts items that have significance in their family community. From tattered blankets to family photos, from dirty, pink casts to worn out cat collars, the students share heartfelt possessions and memories that make their family community and personal history unique. In addition, they give classmates a glimpse of what is treasured, important, and even sacred in various families.

As a culminating activity we invite parents, siblings, and grandparents to our Keepsakes Roadshow. This is our version of the *Antiques Roadshow,* but rather than trying to determine if an item is worth a fortune, the students teach the parents about their valuable keepsakes, stories, and learning. The students become curators of their own social studies museum, set up shop, and share their expertise. Parents are free to explore the room and question each expert about his or her memory box, name history, or family recipe. Because the unit is highly personal, all students, regardless of academic ability, are able to participate fully and with great confidence. Better yet, the parents catch the excitement the children are feeling and become strong supporters of their child's learning. Perhaps most important, since the children experience personal success, they are anxious to gain knowledge and look forward to more active learning in social studies throughout the year.

My job is not just to teach and test the curriculum standards and benchmarks. My responsibility is far more important: I must teach children and inspire a love of learning. In my classroom, that cannot be done by merely reading a textbook. Instead, learning must occur in an active, engaging way, so all students feel a personal connection with the topic and expand their expertise.

Helpful Tips

■ When conducting a Keepsakes Roadshow, make sure to include a dress rehearsal prior to the big evening. We generally invite a neighboring classroom in to view our exhibits and ask questions. This helps the students polish their act before parents arrive that evening.

■ When parents arrive, it is appropriate to provide them with a roadmap of suggested questions. I've found that parents

---

(Continued)

take this evening quite seriously and want to question the students appropriately; however, they usually seem a little leery about getting started. Providing them with sample questions gets them going and leads to an enjoyable evening for parents and students alike.

■ Social studies seems to tie in beautifully to the language arts curriculum. While completing this unit in social studies, my students read stories about families; those by Tommie dePaola and Patricia Polacco are especially fitting. The children also write their own autobiographies and create a Picasso-style self-portrait. These activities address different learning styles and extend the importance of personal history into other areas of the curriculum.

CHAPTER **8**

Reaching Students Through Fine Arts

 When Problems of Poverty Interfere With Schooling: Music as a Path to Success

Stephen Lin
Louisville, Kentucky

The love of music has brought many levels of students to my class, and I strive to make the class challenging for everyone. I feel that I inspire the students to be successful through rehearsal and performance by demonstrating the passion and emotion of music. A day without a passionate musical rehearsal is like the class not meeting at all. We work together to increase their vocal and sight-reading abilities and their knowledge of music theory and cultural diversity, and I encourage them to explore their own emotions involving interpretation of music as a language.

What continually motivates me to teach music and explore its relationship to life is best illustrated by one of my students. I discovered a ninth-grade student with a promising voice in one of my beginning choruses. She was from an economically deprived neighborhood in our city and had not done well in school. She auditioned for my top choir, the Chamber Singers, and shocked everyone in the school who knew her when she passed the audition. Although she was only a sophomore, the other Chamber Singers accepted and encouraged her to work hard both musically and academically, and she moved from the comprehensive program to the honors program of our school. In her junior year, she moved from the honors program to the advanced program. Her interaction with and influence from students who were in the advanced program motivated her to achieve academically, even though she had not experienced academic success before her sophomore year. In her senior year she was motivated to sing and did as well as she could academically, and she soon had offers from colleges.

I trained this student and watched her grow to become a good singer, and she made the Kentucky All State Chorus three times. Other students encouraged her to work hard and helped her earn the money to attend our international concert tours. She probably will not have opportunities for foreign travel with her friends for some time; she now encourages new students to work hard in music and in academics, so they might have the same results. To watch her develop as a musician with a deeper understanding of musical style and culture and as a person with new dreams and academic goals has been one of the most rewarding experiences for me.

Music is an integral and academic part of education and should serve as enrichment to the total development of the student. Every student should be given the opportunity to learn, succeed, and perform music or work in other fine art forms, because through arts education and activities students learn the process of working together. A systematic approach to solving problems and developing self-control is provided in the music rehearsal. This systematic approach may be carried over to other academic classes as a way to solve problems and conduct research. Music provides opportunities to evaluate aesthetic behavior and performance, and it creates a desire to participate in high-quality performance. Various music experiences help to develop respect and appreciation of different musical forms and cultural diversity.

I have been fortunate to have students respond to the good vibrations of music. My choirs have toured all over the world, spreading the excitement of music. Because of active involvement from parents and students, fundraising, and grants, my choirs have traveled to Belgium, Brazil, Canada, the Czech Republic, France, Greece, Germany, Great Britain, Holland, Iceland, Ireland, Japan, New Zealand, Russia, and Switzerland. Because we travel internationally, the students make every effort to learn multicultural music. Our choirs perform music in a country's original language. We have sung in several African dialects, Chinese, Czech, French, Icelandic, German, Hebrew, Latin, Japanese, Krao (native Brazil Indians), Maori, Portuguese, Romanian, Russian, Samoan, Spanish, and Swedish. Once students learn the original language along with learning about the culture, they have a better understanding of how the language and music interact.

On a choir tour to Rio de Janeiro, Brazil, I instructed my students to become teachers of music as we worked with underprivileged students in a combined elementary and middle school. The choir performed and provided some instruction to students who had never experienced formal choral instruction. They became ambassadors of education as they used their talents and practiced what they had been taught at home. They realized the level of commitment involved in our program, the amount of time and effort. The rewards, the good vibrations, came from seeing those students in Brazil succeed in singing. My good vibrations came from seeing my students succeed as young teachers. After that experience, several of my students expressed a desire to become music teachers. I have encouraged my students to be teachers only if they plan to become fully involved with the passion of music and the excitement of teaching.

Project Van Go: An Art Outreach to Remote and Rural Schools

Jennifer Williams
Nampa, Idaho

I am involved in a program in which high school students become teachers for the day, preparing and presenting art lessons. Many of these students are at risk, struggling with personal and social issues. This project provides many benefits: It promotes the high schoolers' self-esteem and brings art to disenfranchised schools that do not have the benefit of art teachers or art supplies.

Story 1

"Mrs. Inama can't come to the phone," squeals a third-grade student, answering a call from the school district office. "She's plastered!" says the student. It had begun as a very challenging morning at the Atlanta School, located in the Sawtooth Mountains of Idaho. We were traveling on one of our Van Go trips (so named because I put students in my van and we go). Following us in a rented vehicle was a local photographer, who had been hired to follow the activities of our day and to record, in photos, the rather unconventional teaching practices of our project for a national publication. Typical of early morning trips, my van held five sleepy high school students, who on a normal day wouldn't get up this early for anyone. However, today was different.

Project Van Go made them feel needed, fulfilled, and exhausted, and took them to places they had never seen before. It was worth the sacrifice of extra sleep. Several students napped until we turned from the paved highway onto the dirt road that would take us to the Atlanta School. Seventeen miles doesn't seem like much unless you are in a traffic jam on the Bay Bridge in Oakland, California, or on a winding, dusty, potholed road, with the sun in your face. Never mind that it was logging season, and the only way you knew a truck was coming was to keep your window down and listen for the roar as it approached. The combination of dust and vehicles brought visibility to nearly zero. With each turn of the road, one or more students began to feel carsick. Several times we had to stop the car completely. At one juncture, even the photographer was walking off the nausea in the bushes that hugged the narrow road. But the trip was always worth the inherent hazards. For many of the students, this was their first adventure, ever, outside of their town, and they were excited. This particular year, there were only three children enrolled at the Atlanta School, with a fourth child who was only a preschooler. We spent the entire day working on art projects and bonding with the students.

Art is the calling card for so many students, and the interaction of kids is where the true value manifests itself. My high school students became teachers for the day. The second teacher from the tiny school was somebody I knew from previous visits and was a great sport. She let us plaster her face as a preliminary step for making Indian masks. When the phone rang in her tiny classroom, a very innocent voice pronounced that the teacher was "plastered." I decided it was time to take the call myself.

We worked the entire day to bring the rudimentary elements of an art curriculum to this school that had no art teacher and no art supplies. After many thanks and hugs, we began our trip home, which turned out to be about two hours longer than the trip in. It seems that I took a left instead of a right, somewhere, and had to wait out a very curious skunk that circled our van inquisitively. The kids didn't mind. They were feeling full of something that was more spiritual than physical. In fact, they were happy that the excursion to places unknown would continue.

And Just a Side Note . . .

The reporter who wrote the story about our adventure that day published it in a national paper. A teacher in the Midwest read the paper and sent it to her father, a dentist, in Washington State. He, in turn, wrote me a letter and enclosed $100 for Project Van Go. You see, he had been a student long ago at the Atlanta School.

Story 2

After September 11, 2001, and the spring that brought renewed dreams, Secretary of Education Rod Paige asked the nation's schools to stop at exactly noon on a particular day to say the Pledge of Allegiance in unison. It happened that Van Go was on the road again. This time we were at the Pine School, located on the north end of Anderson Ranch Dam, somewhere between Mountain Home Air Force Base and Sun Valley, Idaho (as the crow flies), with their eleven students and my six.

As we worked, we realized that the noon hour was approaching. Almost immediately, the Pine School students began to count down the time from 11:55 A.M. to noon. We gathered on the little playground next to the swing sets, where a small metal flagpole supported an American flag. We were ready to say our pledge. By now my students had bonded with the kids from Pine School, so hand in hand they stood with their favorite new friends. And what a sight we were—nineteen total—with one hand pressed to our heart and the other holding the hand of a student. It was a lovely day, with the sun casting huge shadows from the pine trees that surrounded the school. The countdown ended, and we began the words, "I pledge allegiance . . ." What an incredible moment! We knew a nation was sharing our words at the very same moment. And, as if the pledge was not enough to raise the goose bumps on our arms, we began to sing, a cappella, the national anthem. None of our voices were in unison. We sounded more like a chorus of cackling crows! Nobody there would dispute that we had just made the worst music to our ears but the most beautiful music our hearts had ever heard. One can only imagine what the lone backpacker was thinking as he came from a trail out of the pine trees across the road. This experience bonded our little troop of students for all of eternity. When we left, everyone exchanged addresses and promised to be pen pals.

Story 3

Going to the Almo School, by the city of Rocks in southwestern Idaho, is as much about doing art with little kids as it is about exploring one of the most famous places to rock climb in the world. I spent the morning with my high school students as they presented lessons on color and wax application for a batik and tie-dye project. We were spread from the tiny cafeteria area (where rangers, rock climbers, and ranchers show up for lunch) to the classrooms (two total), hallways, and front steps of the school. And how kids love to get their hands dirty! It seems to be a rite of passage for children to get as dirty as they can when doing art, which is just fine with me. The dye we were using covered aprons and art shirts, and hands were a more beautiful tie-dye than any shirt could ever be. At noon my high school students were playing kickball and tag with their new friends. There were squeals and screams from kids who knew this traditional school day would be extraordinary. For the students of Almo School, mostly kindergarten through eighth-grade students, this was a day to make things with their hands and to socialize with the outside world. Not only do these children not have the benefit of art teachers or art supplies, they also never get to mingle with high school kids or have them as teachers for the day.

One little first-grade boy, Stephen, followed me around the entire day. "Can I do another project?" he'd say. "Can I be the first to play with clay on that spinning thing?" he'd ask, pointing at the portable potter's wheel I brought. He was my shadow, my buddy for certain. It seemed that everyone had a buddy or two that day and on every trip we take. One of the truly wonderful things about Van Go and the trips is that we try to go back to each school at least every other year. This way we attempt to build a small art curriculum, and we can watch the kids grow up. As we were doing our farewell hugs at the end of the day with promises to return as soon as we could, Stephen came running, breathlessly, down the schoolhouse steps. "Hey wait! Here," he said. "You brought me art today, and I want to give you my favorite pencil." Sometimes, we're miles from the school before any of us can speak.

Story 4

The quaint little Ola School looks like something you'd see on a postcard. It is one of the lucky remote schools that contains two classrooms. Nestled on top of a hill, with one general store, a country church, and several movie houses in the vicinity, the town looks like a scene out of an old Norman Rockwell painting. If people want lunch, they can usually find a menu on the chalkboard at the local store. However, don't expect that they'll have what is listed. A chili dog might come without chili, and, though a grilled cheese and tuna is delicious, they may not have the tuna.

We began the day papermaking arid basketry with one classroom before lunch, moving to the second classroom after lunch. Becky was a kindergarten student and both hearing and speech impaired. She was cute and precocious; all of my students wanted to take her home. Not only did she prove to be the best art student, but also she taught us that nothing is impossible. What she lacked in being able to hear, or being able to speak, she communicated with her eyes and her smile and the incredible tactile reaction she had to a vat of watery pulp. My students understood how something as simple as a hornet's nest could give a whole new perspective to a child's view of his or her own world. The Ola School kids knew these nests all too well, but most did not know that the green hornet is the world's greatest papermaker, chewing and regurgitating pulp to make the fine papers of the nest. They also knew that you respected anything that can sting. They have many bees flying around in their schoolyard, and they try to leave them alone since the hornets have been residents of the school's library for more years than most of the kids have been alive. On one of our subsequent visits in the years to come, Becky would be a sixth-grade student. As the students hugged Becky and said good-bye, no words were needed to tell what we meant to each other, what Van Go had brought into her life. Another boy later shared that, with the skills he had learned making natural willow baskets with us several years before, he was now making baskets from the willow around his house and selling them to help with the family finances.

Story 5

Yep, the road was closed, but we never saw the sign. Funny how you don't really think anything is wrong, even though you have to drive around boulders the size of tractors and wind up cow trails to avoid the washed out areas of the road. The 2.5-hour drive, including the flat tire that a girl had to show the boys how to change, was well worth the adventure of finally getting to Yellowpine University, near the Stebnite gold mine. The little students immediately bonded with my high school students and begged to sleep in the schoolhouse with us that night. The Yellowpine students—all six of them—ran from one side of the room to the other. They acted like kids in a candy store after eating too much sugar. They were excited and wanted to do everything at once. Never mind that school got out at 3:00 P.M. We were still doing art at 5:00 that evening, until somebody yelled "Baseball!" and off we went to a grassy, rocky field with my high school students in tow. In between the home-runs and yells of delight that we finally had a complete team, students watched over the pit they had dug for the primitive pottery and the fire that was creating the smoke needed to turn the pots black. Sleeping in the schoolhouse was a treat—and thank goodness for a wood stove.

The next morning our baseball field had turned into a grazing site for a herd of elk. The art projects started almost immediately. Several students were trying not to laugh as they watched the local postman—who had just stopped in to say hello—get his face plastered. The youngest student at Yellowpine exclaimed, "This is the best day of my life! I even did my homework so that I could do art." Nearly all of the Van Go trips become community events. I remember traveling to Jarbidge School in an old gold mining town in Nevada, a very isolated spot. The last seventeen miles into the town winds through breathtaking canyons. One student in the school, which was a converted trailer, said, "Nobody ever comes to see us from the outside . . . except you guys." Joining us were students' family members, their pets, and the town's author, who spends her spring and summer talking and writing about the gold mining days. Talk about a history lesson! She was nearly 80 years old, but she did the art projects alongside my students and shared with us stories from another generation.

Story 6

Prairie School is a one-room red schoolhouse on the prairie. It was the first school that Van Go visited nearly three decades ago. The students then are the parents of the students now. These are kindergarten though eighth-grade students, and many of them drive themselves or ride a horse to school. Always the children are waiting anxiously for us to arrive. We are like family to them. I realized this when I was asked to be the guest speaker at their graduation of two. We've been treated to so much when we travel to Prairie, including home-baked goods and deep-fried chicken. One time we were taken by one of the grandmothers across an entire volcanic basalt field at the edge of her backyard to look at the areas that the Native Americans had used to sharpen their home-made bows. Coming from the Mountain Home side to Prairie we saw a wonderful granite outcropping where a trail leads to Native American pictographs. Even more exciting was the special education student I brought with me who had never climbed anything until she hiked the trail, holding hands with other students, to view the cave and the painting at the top. It was life changing for her and certainly the biggest challenge she had ever faced.

The Prairie School houses a mural that we've worked on together for twenty years and finally finished. There is no doubt in my mind that the small community of Prairie would circle the school like protective wagons if anybody threatened to paint over it. Prairie was the first school I dared to take several high school kids to. These particular students were so depressed and suicidal that many thought I was crazy to do it. As it happened, these kids became part of the heart of Van Go, becoming some of my better instructors and changing their own lives forever to become more confident and caring human beings, with a positive outlook on life. Perhaps, for the first time in their lives, they were experiencing a new self-image.

They were given responsibilities and taking charge. They were someone to somebody. Prairie has always taught us about the importance of the simple things in life—clean air, an appreciation for nature, and a less harried pace to life. Van Go has traveled to nursing homes, the zoo, and the humane society. It has been to the Red Cross, lockdown facilities for youth, and urban schools. It has been a project that has taken life's lessons beyond classroom walls in a poignant and meaningful way. It bas been a win-win adventure for the thousands of lives it has touched. The best compliment comes from my students, who say that when they grow up, they, too, want to continue the legacy of Van Go.

Helpful Tips

1. It takes a very supportive school, school district, and administration for a project like Van Go to exist.

2. It is possible to find grants and awards to support the efforts of such a project.

3. It takes energy, a vision, an ability to see a need, and guts to undertake a project of such magnitude.

Index

**CORWIN
PRESS**

The Corwin Press logo—a raven striding across an open book—represents the union of courage and learning. Corwin Press is committed to improving education for all learners by publishing books and other professional development resources for those serving the field of K–12 education. By providing practical, hands-on materials, Corwin Press continues to carry out the promise of its motto: **"Helping Educators Do Their Work Better."**